CAMPAIGN 339

# KOS AND LEROS 1943

The German Conquest of the Dodecanese

**ANTHONY ROGERS**

ILLUSTRATED BY DARREN TAN
*Series Editor Marcus Cowper*

OSPREY
Bloomsbury Publishing Plc
PO Box 883, Oxford, OX1 9PL, UK
1385 Broadway, 5th Floor, New York, NY 10018, USA
E-mail: info@ospreypublishing.com
**www.ospreypublishing.com**

OSPREY is a trademark of Osprey Publishing Ltd

First published in Great Britain in 2019

A catalogue record for this book is available from the British Library.

ISBN: PB 9781472835116; eBook 9781472835109; ePDF 9781472835093;
XML 9781472835123

19 20 21 22 23 10 9 8 7 6 5 4 3 2 1

Maps by Bounford.com
3D BEVs by The Black Spot
Index by Nick Hayhurst
Typeset by PDQ Digital Media Solutions, Bungay, UK
Printed in China through World Print Ltd.

## DEDICATION

In memory of Giannis Paraponiaris

## ACKNOWLEDGEMENTS

In addition to those whose images are individually credited, I also wish to
thank and acknowledge Jürgen Bernhagen, Clifford Clark, Judy Chatterton
Dickson, Hans Peter Eisenbach, Walter Keller and his daughter Ulla Häfner,
Ted and Ruth Johnson, Barbara Kuhlmann, Roger Leverette, Walter
Lünsmann and his daughter Uschi Lohmann, Peter Schenk, Thorsten
Schnaars, Derek Sullivan, Garry Symonds, Theodore Theodorou, Uwe
Wilhelm Walther and family of the late Hansjürgen Weissenborn.

## TIME ZONES

Between September and November 1943, Allied forces in the Aegean
operated under various time zones including Greenwich Mean Time (GMT)
and time zones A, B and C. Time zone A (-1) was one hour ahead of GMT; B
(-2) and C (-3) were two and three hours ahead of GMT respectively. The
Germans kept to time zone B until 0200hrs on 4 October 1943, when those
in and around Kos switched to time zone A. The British, on the other hand,
seem to have been less consistent, although on Kos units adhered mainly
to time zone C. By November, the British were operating under time zone B.
For consistency, time zone C (-3) is used whenever possible up to 31
October 1943 and time zone B (-2) thereafter.

Osprey Publishing supports the Woodland Trust, the UK's leading woodland
conservation charity. Between 2014 and 2018 our donations are being
spent on their Centenary Woods project in the UK.

To find out more about our authors and books, visit
**www.ospreypublishing.com**. Here you will find extracts, author
interviews, details of forthcoming events and the option to sign up for
our newsletter.

**Key to military symbols**

| | | | | | | |
|---|---|---|---|---|---|---|
| XXXXX Army Group | XXXX Army | XXX Corps | XX Division | X Brigade | III Regiment | II Battalion |
| I Company/Battery | ••• Platoon | •• Section | • Squad | Infantry | Artillery | Cavalry |
| Airborne | Unit HQ | Air defence | Air Force | Air mobile | Air transportable | Amphibious |
| Anti-tank | Armour | Air aviation | Bridging | Engineer | Headquarters | Maintenance |
| Medical | Missile | Mountain | Navy | Nuclear, biological, chemical | Ordnance | Parachute |
| Reconnaissance | Signal | Supply | Transport movement | Rocket artillery | Air defence artillery | |

**Key to unit identification**

Unit identifier — Parent unit
Commander
(+) with added elements
(−) less elements

Ju 52s convey paratroopers of 15./4.Rgt. 'Brandenburg' during
a low-level approach to Astipalaea on 22 October 1943. (BA:
101I-525-2299-20A)

# CONTENTS

**INTRODUCTION**                                                             4
The strategic setting

**CHRONOLOGY**                                                               8

**OPPOSING COMMANDERS**                                                      9
German commanders . British commanders . Italian commanders

**OPPOSING FORCES**                                                         13
German forces . British forces . Italian forces . Order of battle

**OPPOSING PLANS**                                                          20
German plans . British plans

**THE CAMPAIGN**                                                            25
Prelude . Operation *Eisbär* . War at sea and on land: 4–11 October
War at sea: 12–21 October . Levitha . War at sea: 22–31 October
Change of command at Leros . War at sea and in the air: 1 – 11 November
Enigma and *Ultra* . Operation *Taifun* 12 November . 13 November
14 November . 15 November . 16 November

**THE AFTERMATH**                                                           90

**THE BATTLEFIELDS TODAY**                                                  92

**BIBLIOGRAPHY**                                                            93

**INDEX**                                                                   95

# INTRODUCTION

During World War I, Winston Churchill had been forced to resign as First Sea Lord of the Admiralty as a result of his role in the disastrous Allied effort in the Dardanelles. Twenty-eight years on, his apparent fixation with the region would resurface with dire consequence. The Italian armistice of September 1943 provided Churchill, now Britain's prime minister, with an opportunity to conduct a major operation in the eastern Mediterranean. It was argued that a new front in the Aegean would increase pressure against a faltering Wehrmacht and might even persuade Turkey to join the Allies. In spite of American opposition, Churchill proceeded. Spearheaded by the Special Boat Squadron and the Long Range Desert Group, British-led forces were sent to occupy the Italian-administered Dodecanese. Three months later, Kastellorizo was the only island remaining in British hands. The cost was an entire infantry brigade, some 100 aircraft and 20 naval vessels.

## THE STRATEGIC SETTING

The Aegean Sea is part of the eastern Mediterranean and provides access via the Dardanelles to the Sea of Marmara. This, in turn, is linked by

The Germans were quick to react in the wake of the Italian armistice. Generalleutnant Ulrich Kleeman's Sturmdivision Rhodos seized control of Rhodes on 11 September 1943, taking prisoner some 35,000–40,000 Italians. A vast quantity of Italian weapons was also seized. (Author's collection)

On Monday morning, 13 September, an advance party of the Special Boat Squadron arrived by sea at Kos. These are members of 'S' Detachment SBS and crew of ML 349 at Kos port. (Kostas Kogiopoulos)

the Bosporus to the Black Sea. The Aegean is characterized by its many islands, with two main archipelagos forming the Cyclades in the south, and the Dodecanese in the south-east. The Dodecanese, populated mainly by those of Greek extraction, comprise 14 principal islands (not 12 as the name implies). These are: Patmos, Lipsi, Leros, Kalymnos, Kos, Astipalaea, Nisyros, Tilos, Halki, Symi, Rhodes, Karpathos, Kasos and Kastellorizo.

In the early 16th century, after more than 200 years under the Knights of St John, Rhodes, soon followed by the rest of the Dodecanese, fell to the Ottomans. The situation prevailed until the Italo-Turkish war of 1911–12, from which Italy would emerge triumphant, having seized Libya and most of the Dodecanese. An agreement that Italy would relinquish control in the Dodecanese was delayed by the outbreak of the Balkan Wars (1912–13) and further complicated as a result of World War I, when, as an inducement for the Italians to come on side, the Allies accorded Italy full possession of the Dodecanese. After the Armistice, the future of the region continued to be a subject for debate, but was still under Italian occupation at the start of World War II.

When, in September 1939, Britain and France declared war on Germany, Turkey refrained from taking sides, preferring instead to maintain cordial relations with the warring factions. Il Duce Benito Mussolini also opted for neutrality, until the time seemed right to join what looked like being the winning side. On 10 June 1940, Italy entered the war as Germany's ally against Britain and France.

The Greeks did not wish to precipitate a German invasion by allowing Britain to establish a military presence in their country. But, after meeting with the British Foreign Secretary Anthony Eden in February 1941, Greek government ministers were persuaded that Germany intended in any event to subjugate their homeland. The Royal Navy had already been granted the use of port facilities on the island of Crete and soon British forces began to arrive in mainland Greece. The Germans invaded a few weeks later and by the end of April they had overrun the country. Surviving British and Greek forces withdrew to Crete, which fell to a German airborne assault in May 1941.

Farther south, German forces had recently arrived in Libya in support of their Italian allies. In the central Mediterranean, Malta continued to provide the Royal Air Force and the Royal Navy with a base from which to disrupt Axis supply routes, but was proving expensive to maintain. The situation in North Africa might have developed very differently had Malta not held out. As it was, the outcome of the desert war remained in the balance until mid-1942, by which time British forces had been pushed back towards Alexandria before the line was eventually stabilized at El Alamein.

On 18 October, the final Italo-German air offensive against Malta ended in an Allied victory. On the night of the 23rd, the British Eighth Army launched a major offensive against Axis forces in the Western Desert. It was the beginning of the end for the Deutsches Afrikakorps. October 1942 heralded a welcome reversal of British fortunes in the Mediterranean and the Middle East. By November, the Afrikakorps was retreating westward and on the 8th the Allies landed in Algeria and Morocco.

Now that they were in a position to do so, the commanders-in-chief in the Middle East began to consider action in the eastern Mediterranean. If they could re-occupy Crete and take possession of the Dodecanese, the

Officers of the Kos Allied landing party, probably on their way to meet the Italian commander, Colonello Felice Leggio: Second from left is SBS Major David Sutherland; to his left is Lieutenant Commander Frank Ramseyer, RNVR. (Kostas Kogiopoulos)

British would be ideally placed to restrict Axis movements in the region. Such a development was bound to inspire Turkish confidence and might even persuade Turkey to declare openly for the Allies. This would allow the use of Turkish airbases from which to strike at Greece, Romania and Bulgaria; it would open the way through the Dardanelles and Bosporus and, controversially, could even lead to action in the Balkans. After reconsidering, it was concluded that the defences in Crete were such that it was unlikely that the island could be taken. The possibility of capturing Rhodes and the Dodecanese with the object of opening the Aegean as far as Izmir in Turkey was seen as feasible, but only if the Luftwaffe was pre-occupied elsewhere. There would also be a requirement for additional resources: two auxiliary aircraft carriers, 88 assorted landing craft and ten aircraft squadrons. A proposal was referred to Winston Churchill, then in Morocco attending the Casablanca Conference with America's President Roosevelt. The idea appealed to the Prime Minister, who decided to seek the opinions of the Chiefs of Staff. They needed time to respond. The whole question of Allied strategy for 1943 was still under consideration and depended largely on available resources. But just six days later, on 27 January 1943, Churchill instructed the commanders-in-chief to plan and prepare for the capture of the Dodecanese employing the utmost 'ingenuity and resource'.

The Americans were less than enthusiastic about opening another front. The United States Military Command considered that there was really only one way to defeat Hitler: by striking at Germany itself. Operations in the Aegean, codename 'Accolade', would therefore be almost exclusively a British affair.

On 25 July 1943, following the Allied invasion of Sicily (Operation Husky) Benito Mussolini was ousted and replaced by Maresciallo Pietro Badoglio. Suddenly, it seemed, Italy had no interest in continuing the war as an Axis partner. While Badoglio's government negotiated surrender terms with the Allies, Adolf Hitler and his Staff prepared for the inevitable. Having anticipated Italy's volte-face the Germans responded with countermeasures under the codename Achse (Axis). Sturmdivision Rhodos quickly seized control of Rhodes, the largest and strategically most important island in the Dodecanese, disarming and taking prisoner tens of thousands of Italians. British plans to secure Rhodes with the cooperation of resident Italian forces were thus pre-empted. Rhodes was the key, without which, any attempt to seize and hold the rest of the Dodecanese was likely to fail. Winston Churchill was undeterred. Operation Accolade would proceed regardless and British forces were hurriedly deployed to occupy remaining islands.

For some time, Adolf Hitler had expected such an occurrence, his fears reinforced prior to Husky with a strategy of deception by the British and Americans. German forces in Greece and the Balkans were formidable. The German war effort was partly reliant on natural resources imported from the region. Greece, in particular, was a valuable source of ore, including chrome (used in armoured steel production) and bauxite (from which aluminium was extracted). But more importantly, if Allied air bases were established in the Aegean, the all-important Ploesti oilfields in Romania would be well within reach of bombers and long-range fighters. A British presence in the Aegean could hardly be ignored, therefore, and German forces were tasked with taking immediate action.

# CHRONOLOGY

| | |
|---|---|
| 8 September | Italian armistice announced. |
| 9 September | Three-man liaison team parachutes into Rhodes. |
| 10 September | Two-man liaison team parachutes into Kos. Kastellorizo occupied by Special Boat Squadron (SBS). Unofficial mission arrives at Samos. |
| 11 September | German Sturmdivision Rhodos takes control of Rhodes. |
| 13 September | SBS arrives at Kos. |
| 15 September | Long Range Desert Group (LRDG) spearheads occupation of Leros. First of Durham Light Infantry reaches Kos. |
| 16 September | SBS arrives at Samos. |
| 17 September | Royal Irish Fusiliers (first of four infantry battalions) begin to arrive at Leros. SBS sent to Symi. |
| 22 September | Germans prepare to take Kos and Leros. At about this time, the first contingent of the Royal West Kents lands at Samos. |
| 25 September | LRDG sets up base at Kalymnos. |
| 3 October | Operation *Eisbär* (German invasion of Kos) begins. German forces push swiftly inland. |
| 4 October | Kos in German hands. British evacuate Kalymnos. |
| 7 October | Kalymnos occupied by German forces. |
| 11 October | Symi evacuated by British forces. |
| 22 October | Astipalaea invaded by German forces. |
| 24 October | LRDG detachment overwhelmed in battle at Levitha. |

| | |
|---|---|
| 5 November | Brigadier Robert Tilney takes over command on Leros. |
| 12 November | Germans begin Operation *Taifun* with sea landings on the northern coast of Leros and a parachute drop in the centre of the island. Leros is effectively divided in two by German forces. |
| 13 November | More German forces are landed at Leros. German assault takes Appetici. Fighting at Quirico. |
| 13–14 November | Unsuccessful night counter-attack by British at Appetici. |
| 14 November | Clidi is retaken by the Buffs. Fighting resumes at Rachi and at Quirico. Both sides land reinforcements. |
| 15 November | Fighting continues on Rachi Ridge. More British and German reinforcements arrive at Leros. |
| 16 November | Brigadier Tilney is taken prisoner at Meraviglia and surrenders British forces on Leros. |
| 19 November | Allies begin evacuation of Samos. |
| 22 November | Samos is occupied by German forces. With the exception of Kastellorizo, the Dodecanese are in German hands. |

# OPPOSING COMMANDERS

## GERMAN COMMANDERS

**Generaloberst Alexander Löhr** was Commander-in-Chief (C-in-C) Heeresgruppe E (Army Group E), which controlled the Wehrmacht (German armed forces) in the Aegean area. The Kriegsmarine (German Navy) in the eastern Mediterranean was nowhere near as powerful as the Royal Navy's Mediterranean Fleet, but nonetheless crucial to German operations in the region. Senior naval officer Aegean was **Vizeadmiral Werner Lange**. Air operations fell to **General der Flieger Martin Fiebig** of Luftwaffenkommando Südost (Air Force Command South-East). Land forces were the responsibility of **Generalleutnant Friedrich-Wilhelm Müller**, a Prussian officer who, like many of his generation, had fought in World War I. Since 1939, he had served on the Western and Eastern Fronts. In autumn 1943 he was Commanding Officer (CO) of 22. Infanteriedivision, from which the majority of troops were drawn for forthcoming operations in the Dodecanese.

Land forces were organized into several *Kampfgruppen* (battle groups). For the taking of Kos, there would be two such groups. Each was named

**LEFT**
Generalleutnant Friedrich-Wilhelm Müller commanded 22. Infanteriedivision, whose troops comprised the majority of land forces tasked with seizing the Dodecanese. During operations to take Kos and Leros, Müller's assault force was organized into several *Kampfgruppen* (battle groups). For Operation *Eisbär* there were two such groups, each named after its respective commander. (Author's collection)

**FAR LEFT**
Major Sylvester von Saldern officer commanding II./Gren.-Rgt. 65 was responsible for Kampfgruppe von Saldern during Operations *Eisbär* and *Taifun*. (Author's collection)

9

after its respective commander. **Major Sylvester von Saldern** was the experienced CO of II. Bataillon/Grenadierregiment 65 (II./Gren.Rgt. 65) and Kampfgruppe von Saldern. (In the Wehrmacht, Roman numerals were used to indicate battalions, and Arabic numerals other unit formations.) **Hauptmann Armin Kuhlmann** was born in Namibia, a dual German and British national. He is thought to have served in an infantry unit in Poland in 1939 and, later, in North Africa. He was officer commanding (OC) 1. Kompanie/Küstenjägerabteilung 'Brandenburg' (1./Küstenjäger-Abt. 'Brandenburg') and Kampfgruppe Kuhlmann.

Five battle groups were created for the seizure of Leros. Tasked once again was Kampfgruppe von Saldern, as well as Brandenburg Küstenjäger. This time, however, the latter would land as Kampfgruppe Schädlich under

**Leutnant Hans Schädlich,** who had succeeded Hauptmann Kuhlmann after he was severely wounded in an air raid at Kalymnos. **Hauptmann Helmut Dörr** was the very capable CO of III. Bataillon/Grenadierregiment 440 (III./Gren.Rgt. 440) and Kampfgruppe Dörr. There was also an airborne element, Kampfgruppe Kühne, named after **Hauptmann Martin Kühne,** CO of I. Bataillon/Fallschirmjägerregiment 2 (I./Fallschirmjäger-Rgt. 2). As an officer in the paratroopers, Kühne had fought in Holland in 1940 and in Crete in 1941 (being wounded on both occasions), subsequently serving in Russia, North Africa and Italy, before arriving in the Aegean. Finally, there was Kampfgruppe Aschoff, which was led by **Hauptmann Philipp Aschoff,** CO II. Bataillon/Grenadierregiment 16 (II./Gren.Rgt. 16).

Hauptmann Philipp Aschoff OC II./Gren.Rgt. 16 and commander of Kampfgruppe Aschoff. (Author's collection)

# BRITISH COMMANDERS

Naval forces in the Aegean and at Kastellorizo fell to the C-in-C, Levant, **Admiral Sir John H. D. Cunningham** (succeeded on 14 October 1943 by **Vice Admiral Sir Algernon U. Willis**). **Air Commodore W. H. Dunn** was in charge of air operations and subordinate to the Air Defence commander, **Air Vice Marshal Richard Saul,** in Cairo. **Lieutenant-General Sir Desmond Anderson** was responsible for all army and air forces in the Aegean and at Kastellorizo. Local command of army and air forces in Kastellorizo was vested in **Major Gavin Shaw** (The Welch Regiment). **Colonel Lionel F. R. Kenyon** (Corps of Royal Engineers) was appointed to command all troops on Kos.

Aegean operations were controlled initially by Middle East Command working through III Corps Headquarters (Force 292) and 234 Brigade, the latter under **Brigadier (later Major-General) F. G. R. 'Ben' Brittorous** on Leros. Brittorous had been an infantry officer in the Manchester Regiment in World War I. He had served in France in 1940 before arriving at Malta, where he was CO of 8th (Ardwick) Battalion The Manchester Regiment. He became Fortress Commander on Leros in autumn 1943. When developments dictated the necessity for a separate command to handle operations in the

**BELOW LEFT**
Vizeadmiral Werner Lange steps ashore at Salamis to inspect naval forces shortly prior to the commencement of operations in the Aegean. (Author's collection)

**BELOW RIGHT**
At the conclusion of the battle for the Aegean, the commander of Luftwaffenkommando Südost, General der Flieger Martin Fiebig (left), converses with a Luftwaffe officer, probably Major Bernhard Hamester of Schlachtgeschwader 3. Facing the camera is Geschwaderkommodore, Oberst Kurt Kuhlmey. (Author's collection)

area, **Major-General H. R. Hall** was appointed General Officer Commanding Aegean. Hall established his headquarters on Samos while at the same time, **Brigadier R. A. G. 'Dolly' Tilney** took over from Brittorous on Leros. Tilney was a Royal Artillery officer, and as such considered by some a curious choice as commander of an infantry brigade.

To combat German forces on the ground there were four infantry battalions and various support units. On Kos, there was 1st Battalion The Durham Light Infantry (**Lieutenant-Colonel Robert F. Kirby**). On Leros, there would eventually be 2nd Battalion The Royal Irish Fusiliers (Faughs) (**Lieutenant-Colonel Maurice French**), 4th Battalion The Royal East Kent Regiment (The Buffs) (**Lieutenant-Colonel Douglas P. Iggulden**), 2nd Battalion The Queen's Own Royal West Kent Regiment (**Lieutenant-Colonel B. D. Tarleton**) and 1st Battalion The King's Own Royal Regiment (Lancaster) (**Lieutenant-Colonel S. A. F. S. Egerton**). The Long Range Desert Group (**Lieutenant-Colonel J. R. Easonsmith**) provided a small but very effective force, sometimes in conjunction with a contingent of the Special Boat Squadron (**Major George P. J. R. Jellicoe**).

# ITALIAN COMMANDERS

**Ammiraglio Inigo Campioni** was governor of the Italian Aegean islands, with his headquarters on Rhodes. Subordinate to Campioni were officers responsible for island garrison forces. **Colonnello Felice Leggio** was the senior officer on Kos. **Contrammiraglio Luigi Mascherpa** was the senior officer on Leros. With some exceptions, notably on the islands of Rhodes and Kos, Italian forces would play a comparatively minor role in hostilities.

# OPPOSING FORCES

## GERMAN FORCES

For the first four years of World War II, the Dodecanese were mainly an Italian responsibility. About 35,000–40,000 Italians, later joined by some 7,000–7,500 troops of the German Sturmdivision Rhodos, occupied Rhodes. The latter had evolved from Sturmbrigade Rhodos, formed in March 1943 with units of 22. Infanteriedivision, Grenadierregiment Rhodos and units of 999. Afrikadivision.

Crete, to the south-west, although not part of the Dodecanese, dominated the southern approaches to the Aegean. German forces had been established there since mid-1941. In the wake of the Italian armistice, the Germans wasted no time in taking full control of the island. However, any such move in the Dodecanese was pre-empted by the rapid deployment of British forces. A significant British presence was established on Kastellorizo, Kos and Leros. Kastellorizo, at the southern extremity of the Dodecanese, was of little interest to the Germans. Kos and Leros, however, were more centrally situated and represented a very real threat.

Two German battle groups were deemed sufficient for taking Kos. Kampfgruppe von Saldern comprised II./Gren.Rgt. 16 (along with one Pionier platoon), II./Gren.Rgt. 65, III./Gren.Rgt. 440, 3. and 4. Batterien/Artillerieregiment 22 (3. and 4./Art.Rgt. 22), 3. Batterie/Flakbataillon 22 (3./Fla.Btl. 22) and 2. Kompanie/ Pionierbataillon 22 (2./Pi.Btl. 22) less one platoon.

A second battle group was put together with elements of the Division Brandenburg. This special operations unit had been established in October 1939 under the aegis of Amt Ausland/Abwehr im Oberkommando der Wehrmacht, commonly referred to as Abwehr – Germany's military intelligence service. The small force rapidly expanded to become a company, then a battalion and, by June 1940, a regiment, seeing action on all

Leros during the Italian occupation: the island was heavily fortified with coastal, anti-aircraft and dual-purpose gun batteries. This is a 76/40 gun position at Mt Scumbarda. (Archivio Centrale dello Stato)

Units of the Division Brandenburg were widely deployed in the Dodecanese. These *Küstenjäger* officers are shown atop Appetici, Leros, on 16 November 1943. From left: Leutnant Voigts, Oberstabsarzt Martin Schrägle and Leutnant Hans Schädlich (wearing non-regulation Italian navy blue trousers). Both Schrägle and Schädlich were slightly wounded. (Author's collection)

fronts. Sonderverband Brandenburg, as it was known after November 1942, was further reorganized in April 1943, this time as the Division Brandenburg, and became directly responsible to the Chef des Wehrmachtführungsstabes (Chief of the Armed Forces Operations Staff), Genobst. Alfred Jodl. As the war continued, clandestine operations seem to have been scaled down, with the majority of Brandenburger deployed in a more conventional role, as infantry, coastal raiders, paratroopers and in ongoing anti-partisan operations. During Operation *Eisbär*, paratroopers of 15. Kompanie (Fallschirmjäger)/ 4. Regiment 'Brandenburg' (15./4.Rgt. 'Brandenburg') commanded by Oblt. Oschatz, and coastal raiders of 1./Küstenjäger-Abt. 'Brandenburg' would deploy as Kampfgruppe Kuhlmann.

As with British formations, the number of personnel in units could vary. For example, just prior to the battle for Kos, the complement of 5. Kompanie of Grenadierregiment 65 was two officers and 157 other ranks. III. Bataillon of Grenadier Regiment 440, however, deployed with just 250 men. A rough estimate of the total number of those who landed on Kos on 3 October 1943 would be 1,550 all ranks.

The invasion force was transported aboard the steamships *Trapani*, *Catherine Schiaffino*, *Kari*, *Ingeborg* and *Citta di Savona*. Landing craft consisted of nine or ten Marinefährprähme (M.F.P. or F-lighters). There were also three Pioniersturmboote (two of which would be available on the day). As escort vessels there were the minelayers *Drache* and *Bulgaria*, five Unterseebootjäger (U-Jäger were seized enemy vessels taken on by the Kriegsmarine as so-called submarine hunters), three motor boats, two Kriegsfischkutter (K.F.K. or motor fishing vessels) and four G.A.-Boote (coast defence vessels) under the command of 21. Unterseebootjagdflottille (21. U.-Jagdflottille), as well as three Räumboote (minesweepers) of 12. Räumbootflottille (12. R.-Flottille).

Infantrymen, almost certainly II./Gren.Rgt. 65, parade at Suda, Crete, just prior to embarking for the German invasion of Kos. (Author's collection)

In order to take Leros, Generallt. Müller's combat troops were organized into three sub-divisions. The eastern landing force comprised Kampfgruppe Schädlich, with 1./Küstenjäger-Abt. 'Brandenburg'; Kampfgruppe von Saldern, consisting of II./Gren.Rgt. 65, II. Bataillon/Luftwaffen-Jägerregiment 22 (II./Lw.-Jäger-Rgt. 22) and 2./Pi.Btl. 22, and Kampfgruppe Dörr with III./Gren.Rgt. 440. The western landing force, or Kampfgruppe Aschoff, was provided by II./Gren.Rgt. 16. The third, airborne, element, Kampfgruppe Kühne, comprised Luftwaffe paratroopers of I./Fallschirmjäger-Rgt. 2.

A second wave with 3./Fla.Btl. 22 and 3. and 4./Art.Rgt. 22 together with heavy weapons of II./Gren.Rgt. 16 and II./Gren.Rgt. 65. III. Bataillon/Jägerregiment 1 'Brandenburg' (III./1. Rgt. 'Brandenburg') and Fallschirmjäger of 15./4.Rgt. 'Brandenburg' was held in reserve near Athens.

The Kriegsmarine and recently arrived Pionierlandungskompanie 780 (Pi.Ldgs.Kp. 780) were responsible for most of the sea-going transport (the exception were two Pioniersturmboote of the Brandenburg Küstenjäger). Close escort was to be provided by 12. R.-Flottille, 21. U.-Jagdflottille and a number of G.A.-Boote, with additional support by three destroyers of 9. Torpedobootflotille (9. T-Flotille). As landing craft, there were five F-lighters, nine or ten Pionierlandungsboote (Pi-La-Boote) and a lead Pi-Führungsboot, as well as two Küstenjäger Pioniersturmboote.

According to a German report, the operation involved 2,000 personnel including 200 naval crewmen. This would appear to be an underestimate, with 2,300 a more likely figure for ground forces alone.

Air supremacy was crucial to the seizure of both Kos and Leros. On 31 August 1943, Luftwaffe South Eastern Command is thought to have had available 271 serviceable aircraft, of which 215 were located in the Greece/Aegean area and comprised: 43 Messerschmitt Bf 109s (reconnaissance and fighters); nine

Kos was suitable for landing troops, vehicles and heavy weapons. This is a 7.5cm Pak 40 (anti-tank gun) under tow during the advance through Kos. (Author's collection)

Messerschmitt Bf 110s (reconnaissance); 19 Junkers Ju 88s (reconnaissance and fighters); 68 Junkers Ju 87s (dive-bombers); 41 Junkers Ju 52s (transports); 34 Arado Ar 196s and one Blohm und Voss Bv 138 (coastal aircraft). By 10 November, two days before the invasion of Leros, the total number of serviceable aircraft in the region was thought to be 283, including 75 Ju 52 transports.

# BRITISH FORCES

2nd Battalion The Royal Irish Fusiliers (2 RIrF, also known as the Faughs) and 2nd Battalion The Queen's Own Royal West Kent Regiment (2 RWK) had served on Malta throughout the island siege, which began on 11 June 1940 and continued until 20 November 1942. 1st Battalion The Durham Light Infantry (1 DLI) had arrived at Malta from Egypt in early 1942. In June 1943, all three battalions were shipped to the Middle East for re-training in preparation for the intended assault on Rhodes. 1 DLI would instead be deployed to Kos, the Faughs and 2 RWK to Leros. 4th Battalion The Royal East Kent Regiment (4 Buffs) had served in Malta from November 1940 until leaving for Egypt in September 1943. Instead of being deployed as expected for the Italian campaign, the battalion was shipped to Leros. 1st Battalion The King's Own Royal Regiment (1 KORR) was also shipped to Leros. 1 KORR was a composite unit comprising remnants of 1st Battalion The South Wales Borderers, 1st Battalion The Duke of Cornwall's Light Infantry and 1 King's Own; all of which had suffered heavy casualties, mainly during the fighting in North Africa.

On 11 September 1943, 11 Battalion The Parachute Regiment (11 PARA), two detachments of the Special Boat Squadron (SBS), two squadrons of the Long Range Desert Group (LRDG), the

Greek Sacred Squadron (GSS, formed in the previous year with officers of the Royal Hellenic Army), one troop of 133 Light Anti-Aircraft Battery Royal Artillery (133 LAA Bty), and the Kalpaks came under the operational command of Force 292. (Contemporary accounts portray the Kalpaks as a particularly ruthless small force of indigenous fighters under the command of a British officer.) The remainder of the SBS, LRDG Headquarters and Headquarters Raiding Forces remained under General Headquarters in Cairo. Soon after, Raiding Forces became an umbrella organization for the SBS, LRDG, and the Holding Unit, Special Forces (which included officers and men of 30 Commando), the GSS, Kalpaks, 42nd Motor Launch Flotilla and the Levant Schooner Flotilla, with command and control exercised by Headquarters Raiding Forces, Aegean, under Colonel (later Brigadier) D. J. T. Turnbull.

The SBS together with the LRDG spearheaded the British effort to take over the Dodecanese. An Advance HQ and A Company of 11 PARA subsequently made an unopposed drop on Kos preparatory to the arrival on 15 September of the first contingent of 1 DLI. The paratroopers did not remain on Kos. The DLI did and was joined by gunners of 1st Anti-Aircraft Regiment Royal Artillery (1st LAA Regt, with 40mm Bofors), 2909 Squadron of the Royal Air Force Regiment (2909 Sqn RAF Regt, with 20mm Hispano cannon), as well as Spitfire Vs and ground staff of 7 (South African Air Force) Squadron, joined later by an additional eight Spitfires of 74 Squadron.

On 2 October, the day before Kos was invaded, there remained only a few serviceable Spitfires, by which time, air force personnel numbered around 500, including more than 200 RAF Regiment (2909 Sqn and newly

Most of the British garrison in the Dodecanese had previously served on Malta as part of 234 Infantry Brigade. Lieutenant Clifford Clark of 2nd Battalion The Royal West Kent Regiment was awarded the Military Cross on Malta. When Leros fell, he succeeded in evading capture and reaching Turkey. He is seen here manning twin Lewis guns at defence post LQ8, at Malta's Luqa airfield. (Author's collection)

Officers of 2nd Battalion The Royal Irish Fusiliers at Malta on St Patrick's Day, 1943, shortly before deploying to the Middle East and, ultimately, Leros. The commanding officer, Lieutenant-Colonel Maurice French, is seated in the front row, eighth from left. (Author's collection)

Allied naval units comprised British, Greek and Polish warships and submarines. BYMS 72 (seen at the time of launch at New York on 7 April 1943) was severely damaged during the night of 11–12 November 1943 before being seized by German forces. (Author's collection)

arrived reinforcements of 2901 Sqn). There were some 540 DLI, plus RA and support elements.

The first garrison troops to reach Leros were an advance party of the Faughs. The remainder of the battalion followed shortly afterwards. B Company of 2 RWK, which had provided a garrison force on Kastellorizo, was also dispatched to Leros (other companies would arrive later). 4 Buffs began to arrive on 24 October, to be followed on 5 November by 1 KORR. By this time, the infantry had been joined by 3rd Battery (less one troop) 1st LAA Regt (equipped with 12 Bofors); one troop of Field Artillery (with four 18/25-pdr field guns which had found their way onto Samos after being captured by the Germans in France in 1940), additional detachments of the LRDG and SBS, and supporting sub-units including Royal Army Medical Corps (RAMC) and Royal Engineers (RE): a total of approximately 3,300 officers and men.

Warships and submarines would play an essential role, conveying troops, equipment and supplies, and in conducting offensive operations. At the time of the Italian armistice, Adm Sir John Cunningham, Commander-in-Chief (C-in-C), Levant, had at his disposal six Fleet- and two Hunt-class destroyers (8th and 22nd Destroyer Flotillas), 15 submarines (1st Submarine Flotilla and part of 10th Submarine Flotilla) as well as motor launches, Royal Air Force High Speed Launches, and caiques (traditional Mediterranean sailing boats). By the end of November 1943, Aegean operations would have involved a total of six cruisers and as many as 33 destroyers (including six Greek and one Polish), 17 submarines (including two Polish) and numerous small craft.

Unlike their German opponents, the British had limited air capabilities. Good use was made of available transports such as DC-3 Douglas Dakotas. But, with the exception of two flights of Spitfires on Kos, Allied fighters were based far from where they were needed most. The only other suitable aircraft with the range to cover the operational area were twin-engine Bristol Beaufighters. But very few would be seen over or near Leros.

## ITALIAN FORCES

There were on Kos 3,500–4,000 Italians. These are thought to have comprised the majority of II and III battaglione (battalion) of 10° reggimento di fanteria (infantry regiment) of Divisione 'Regina', together with heavy weapons including 81mm mortars; one compagnia cannoni anticarro (anti-tank company), 10ª compagnia mitraglieri costiera (coastal machine gun company) and 403ª compagnia mitraglieri ex-Milizia Volontaria per la Sicurezza Nazionale (ex-'Blackshirts' machine-gun company); there were three units of 36° raggruppamento: XXXI gruppo artiglieria (artillery group) and LXXXII gruppo artiglieria contraerea (anti-aircraft group), both with three additional batteries, and 136ª batteria of XXIX gruppo. Also available was 295ª batteria mitragliere (with 20mm cannon), and various support units. Even so, the questionable effectiveness of Italian-manned coastal and anti-aircraft batteries convinced the British that they could count only on their own Bofors and Hispanos. These were distributed mainly at Antimachia airfield and in the vicinity of Kos town and port.

Italians on Leros are believed to have totalled some 5,500. Approximately half were dockyard workers and other civilians. Military personnel included I battaglione of 10° reggimento di fanteria of Divisione 'Regina'; 8ª compagnia mitraglieri da posizione costiera; 402ª compagnia mitraglieri ex-Milizia Volontaria per la Sicurezza Nazionale; part of 147ª squadriglia (maritime reconnaissance squadron) equipped with Cant seaplanes, and mainly unarmed workers and survivors of sunken ships. The Italians occupied positions overlooking likely landing areas including the bays of Blefuti, Lakki (where Italian Headquarters was situated), Gurna and Serocampo. They also manned anti-aircraft and coastal defence gun positions. There were on Leros 25 batteries with 107 guns ranging in calibre from 76mm to 152mm, although not all were functioning on 12 November 1943.

# ORDER OF BATTLE

## BRITISH AND DOMINION LAND FORCES: KOS

1st Battalion The Durham Light Infantry
1st Light Anti-Aircraft Regiment (part detached to Leros; Kos
    detachment reinforced on 2 October)
2909 Squadron RAF Regiment
2901 Squadron RAF Regiment (detachment arrived on 2 October)

## BRITISH AND DOMINION LAND FORCES: LEROS

2nd Battalion The Royal Irish Fusiliers (Faughs)
2nd Battalion The Queen's Own Royal West Kent Regiment
    (reinforced during the course of the battle)
4th Battalion The Royal East Kent Regiment (Buffs)
1st Battalion The King's Own Royal Regiment
Long Range Desert Group
Special Boat Squadron (detachment)
1st Light Anti-Aircraft Regiment (incomplete 3 LAA Battery)
Troop of Field Artillery

Also on Kos was a Spitfire flight of seven South African Air Force Squadron and another of 74 Squadron. Air Ministry Experimental Stations (radar) were present on the island (and possibly on Leros). British forces were provided with the necessary support structure, with detachments from various units, including 9 Field Company Madras Sappers and Miners, Royal Army Medical Corps (161 Field Ambulance), Royal Corps of Signals, Royal Army Ordnance Corps, Royal Army Service Corps and Royal Electrical and Mechanical Engineers.

## GERMAN LAND FORCES: KOS

**Kampfgruppe von Saldern**
II. Bataillon/Grenadierregiment 16
II. Bataillon/Grenadierregiment 65
III. Bataillon/Grenadierregiment 440
3. Batterie/Artillerieregiment 22
4. Batterie/Artillerieregiment 22
3. Batterie/Flakbataillon 22

2. Kompanie/Pionierbataillon 22

**Kampfgruppe Kuhlmann**
15. Kompanie (Fallschirmjäger)/4. Regiment 'Brandenburg'
1. Kompanie/Küstenjägerabteilung 'Brandenburg'

## GERMAN LAND FORCES: LEROS

**Kampfgruppe Schädlich**
1. Kompanie/Küstenjägerabteilung 'Brandenburg'

**Kampfgruppe von Saldern**
II. Bataillon/Grenadierregiment 65
II. Bataillon/Luftwaffen-Jägerregiment 22
2. Kompanie/Pionierbataillon 22

**Kampfgruppe Dörr**
III. Bataillon/Grenadierregiment 440

**Kampfgruppe Aschoff**
II. Bataillon/Grenadierregiment 16

**Kampfgruppe Kühne**
I. Bataillon/Fallschirmjägerregiment 2

**Second wave (did not land during the battle)**
3. Batterie/Flakbataillon 22
3. Batterie/Artillerieregiment 22
4. Batterie/Artillerieregiment 22
II. Bataillon/Grenadierregiment 16 (heavy weapons only)
II. Bataillon/Grenadierregiment 65 (heavy weapons only)

**Reserve**
III. Bataillon/Jägerregiment 1 'Brandenburg'
15. Kompanie (Fallschirmjäger)/4. Regiment 'Brandenburg'

# OPPOSING PLANS

## GERMAN PLANS

On 23 September 1943, Generallt. Friedrich-Wilhelm Müller, commanding 22. Infanteriedivision, was ordered by Heeresgruppe E to make preparations for the seizure of Kos and Leros. Owing to its importance as an Allied airbase, Kos was selected as the first objective under the codename *Unternehmen Eisbär* (Operation *Polar Bear*). Müller intended to take the island in a surprise assault. A long, narrow beach at Marmari on the north coast was chosen as the landing site for his staff and Kampfgruppe von Saldern. The main road running north-east to south-west along much of the island's length was to be secured as quickly as possible.

II./Gren.Rgt. 16 with one Pionier platoon under the former's CO, Hptm. Philipp Aschoff, was to come ashore on the steep south coast, below Point 428 (Eremita), with the primary task of seizing Italian gun emplacements south of Platani, thus preventing their being trained on Kos town and port and the north-western coast. Because the mountainous terrain on the southern coast was unsuitable for vehicles, the battalion 7.5cm Paks (Panzerabwehrkanonen – anti-tank guns), tow-trucks and extra ammunition were to come ashore with Kampfgruppe von Saldern. Until the two groups could link up, II./Gren. Rgt. 16 would have to rely on mules as a means of transport.

A beach landing and paratrooper deployment were to take place in the narrow southern coastal strip just east of Cape Tigani by Brandenburg forces of Kampfgruppe Kuhlmann. After securing the main objective, Antimachia, the Brandenburger were to marry up with Kampfgruppe von Saldern, pushing south-east towards Antimachia and north-west to Kos town.

The invasion of Leros was initially given the codename *Leopard*. When this was compromised, it was changed to *Taifun* (*Typhoon*). Leros was quite different to Kos. An unusual feature of the island was its many gun batteries. Those planning the operation assumed that the guns could target the entire island, and that potential landing sites along the coast were especially well covered. It was also expected that vulnerable stretches of coastline were fortified and mined. To minimize losses, the obvious beaches at Alinda and Gurna bays were ignored and a number of less likely landing sites selected. It was intended for the first wave to secure these locations and to neutralize local defensive positions. Although assault troops would be only lightly armed pending the proposed arrival of heavy weapons with the second wave, they could rely on air support throughout the operation. Close inter-service co-operation was crucial.

On the map (German labels):

Zeichenerklärung:
- Batteriestellung, 4 Geschütze
- Schwere Flak, 4 Geschütze
- leichte Flak
- Kleinkampfanlage
- F.T.-Anlage
- (57m) Höhenangaben, entnommen der Karte Dodekanes 1:25 000 Bl. 7, Leros

German forces were arguably better prepared than the British. On the ground, German officers often seemed more capable and determined to attain objectives according to plan. On the British side, on Leros in particular, there was often uncertainty and confusion. British officers were lucky if they were provided with any kind of map. German officers could rely on suitable maps, as well as excellent aerial images with key points clearly indicated. (Author's collection)

The original battle plan had allowed for both the first and second waves to embark simultaneously, with the latter ready to follow up when required. However, enemy (Allied) action, bad weather and unavoidable delays had reduced the availability of transport vessels for troops and their equipment to five F-lighters; four Infanterieboote (I-Boote); ten Pi-La-Boote (nine of which appear to have taken part in the initial landing); one Pi-Führungsboot and two Küstenjäger Sturmboote. Close escort was to be provided by two R-Boote and three U-Jäger, with up to four destroyers of 9. T-Flotille as support.

This meant there were sufficient craft to embark only the first wave, with the same vessels having to return for the second wave. It was imperative to accomplish the initial assault before daylight but, with a full moon adding to the problems, Y-Time (H-Hour) could not be scheduled any earlier than 0430hrs. In order to reduce further delays, elements of the second wave were transferred to Kalymnos, the nearest German-occupied island to Leros. On X-1 (D-1) the Headquarters staff of Kampfgruppe Müller moved to

Isolavecchia Bay in Kalymnos, location for the command post (CP) during the first stage of the battle. It was intended to transfer the CP to Leros once a beachhead had been established.

Three embarkation points were allocated for assault units. At 2100hours, II./Gren.Rgt. 65 was to be transported from the port of Kos, past the islands of Pserimos and Kalymnos, to rendezvous at nearby Kalolimnos with III./Gren.Rgt. 440, II./Lw.-Jäger-Rgt. 22 and 1. Küstenjägerkompanie – all of which were to depart from Kalymnos harbour at 2200hrs. After continuing to a pre-selected point the combined eastern force was to divide into its individual landing groups for the final approach to Leros. At 2300hrs the western force, namely II./Gren.Rgt. 16, was to proceed from Marmari on the north coast of Kos, along the west coast of Kalymnos towards the island of Telendo, and on to a pre-selected nautical point for the final approach.

Generalleutnant Müller had impressed upon the naval officer commanding the invasion fleet, Korv.Kpt. Dr. Günther Brandt of 21. U.-Jagdflottille, the importance of continuing once the operation had started, regardless of the appearance of British destroyers and irrespective of any losses. An aborted or delayed landing by any of the units could jeopardize everything.

It was planned for assault units to be inserted by landing craft at coves along the northern coast (between Palma Bay and Grifo Bay), below the height of Appetici, and at two points on the southern shore of Gurna Bay. The narrowest part of Leros (between the bays of Alinda and Gurna) was selected as a drop zone. The intention was for a three-pronged thrust towards Meraviglia. In the event, things did not go as intended, with the southern coast landings having to be aborted and instead redirected north.

# BRITISH PLANS

**OPPOSITE**

The British intention to secure Rhodes as a prerequisite to the occupation of other islands of the Dodecanese was pre-empted by a German takeover soon after the Italian armistice. By the end of September 1943, islands dominating the southern approaches to the Aegean Sea were in German hands. British forces were concentrated mainly on Kos and Leros, with a less significant presence on other islands in and around the Dodecanese.

Initially, Rhodes was selected as the primary objective for occupation by predominantly British forces. After the Germans had taken control of the

# Situation in the Dodecanese and neighbouring islands at the end of September 1943

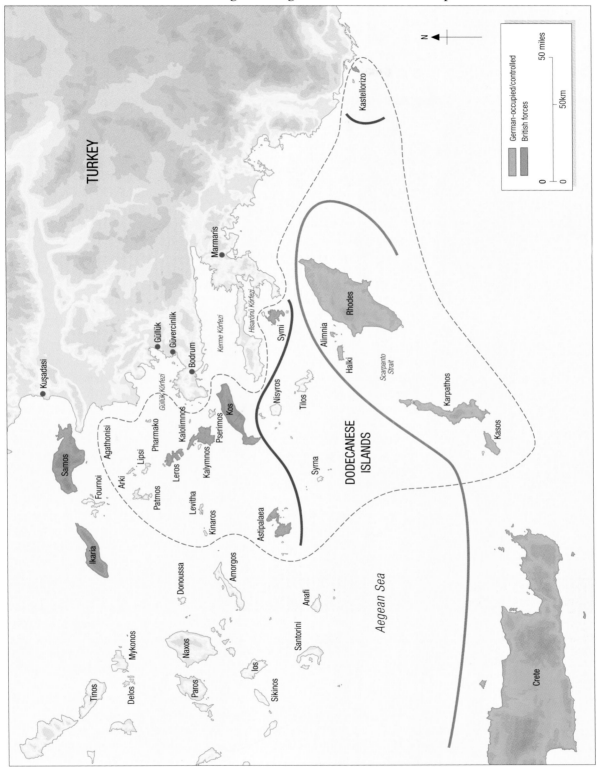

island, attention shifted to Kos and Leros. Kos was essential in that it was suitable as an airbase. Two squadrons each provided a flight of Spitfires. These were based at Antimachia airfield and there were improvised landing grounds on the northern coast. Anti-aircraft defence was the responsibility of army and air force gunners, equipped with 40mm Bofors and 20mm Hispanos respectively. The only available infantry unit was 1 DLI. By October, one company with attached mortars and a section of the Carrier Platoon were assigned to Antimachia airfield. Remaining companies were concentrated in and around Kos town. (On the eve of battle, about 100 personnel of the RAF Regiment also arrived.) Because of its size and importance, one might have expected a more robust island defence. As it was, Kos would be overrun in less than two days.

The final British stand would take place at Leros, where Brig. 'Ben' Brittorous had left the strategy of defence to the CO of the Faughs, Lt. Col. Maurice French. Initially, French had only his own battalion to consider, and concentrated his men on high ground on and around Meraviglia. Lack of numbers precluded wider dispersal, but troops were expected to be able to march to wherever they might be needed. The arrival of reinforcements and a change of command resulted in new arrangements. Acting on instructions of Maj. Gen. Hall, the new Fortress commander, Brig. 'Dolly' Tilney, made himself unpopular by reorganizing the established defence policy, which resulted in the preparation of entirely new positions.

The aim of the revised strategy was to prevent the landing of enemy forces. A problem was lack of transport, which prevented Tilney from maintaining a strong central reserve. So, troops were deployed on a dangerously wide front, thereby aggravating the already poor line of communications. In order to destroy the enemy as quickly as possible, the island was divided into three sectors. The Buffs were deployed in the North, the Faughs (with B Company of the Royal West Kents) in the Centre, and the King's Own (less one company) in the South. Each battalion, with one company held as local reserve, was sited to cover potential landing sites, and units had to be prepared to relocate to other sectors. Fortress reserve (C Company of the King's Own) was held centrally near San Quaranta, with the primary task of counter-attacking paratroopers who might be dropped nearby. Transport – about ten jeeps – was allotted to the company each evening until 'stand down' the following morning.

Medium machine guns were sited to sweep likely landing areas; four 25-pdrs were placed on a feature in the Blacutera area (between San Giovanni and Meraviglia), and 2-pdr anti-tank guns and 40mm Bofors were installed at strategic points in and around the centre of the island. The LRDG manned observation posts (with a wireless link to their headquarters on Meraviglia). A detachment of SBS was also located in low ground between Alinda and Gurna bays. Neither force would be affected by Tilney's changes to the overall defence plan.

Italians were deployed all over Leros and largely responsible for manning the island's gun batteries. The British doubted the loyalty and fighting quality of their new allies, however. Consequently, Italians would play a minor role, enforced by Tilney's decision to restrict their movement when battle commenced.

# THE CAMPAIGN

## PRELUDE

In the race to occupy the Dodecanese and neighbouring islands, both sides made good use of their respective navies. Early on 18 September, two German merchantmen were sunk and an escort vessel was written off during an encounter with Greek and British destroyers. On the 23rd, a German-commandeered steamer with 1,676 Italian prisoners of war was sunk and an escort vessel severely damaged and later sunk by her crew. Allied aircraft also struck at a convoy bound for Crete, accounting for a German transport.

Air cover was crucial for the safe passage of shipping. Aircraft were also indispensable for troop movements and resupply. The Luftwaffe had airfields on Rhodes and Crete as well as in mainland Greece. The only Allied-occupied territory with a suitable landing ground was Kos and, by 17 September, the Germans had been alerted to a British presence on the island.

Aircraft lost during September included, on the 18th, a 216 Squadron Dakota that struck the water during a low-level flight and ditched off Turkey. On board were 1 DLI reinforcements. Passengers and crew survived. Further transports landed at Antimachia and had just been offloaded when Messerschmitt Bf 109s swept across the airfield in a strafing attack, killing and wounding personnel and destroying three Dakotas and badly damaging another. Consequently, remaining DLI would be transported to Kos by sea. Daylight air deliveries were also curtailed, but not in time to prevent two Dakotas from being dispatched from Nicosia on the morning of Sunday the 19th. Within minutes of landing, one machine was burnt out in a strafing attack and one of the crew killed. The other aircraft was refused permission to land and returned with its load to Cyprus. The Dakota damaged in the previous day's raid was hit again, caught fire and burnt out.

On the 18th, 7 (South African Air Force) Squadron also suffered its first combat casualties while operating from Kos. Two Spitfires were shot down offshore. Both pilots were killed. In turn, two Bf 109Gs of IV./Jagdgeschwader 27 (IV./J.G. 27) were lost; one pilot was reported missing and one was taken prisoner. The next day another Spitfire pilot was killed when his fighter crashed after failing to recover from a spin during a dogfight with Bf 109s.

Meanwhile, on 17 September, an advance party of the Faughs had arrived at Leros. More troops and equipment followed. The inevitable German reaction to the British build-up was not long in coming. During an air raid on Lakki port on Sunday morning, 26 September, many were killed when the Greek destroyer *Vasilissa Olga* was sunk. The British destroyer *Intrepid* was

Beaufighters attack a German vessel off the coast of Kos on 3 October 1943. According to the original caption, one of three aircraft had just been shot down. (Author's collection)

severely damaged, sinking the following day. (Within less than a fortnight, the Luftwaffe would also account for at least seven Italian vessels.)

At Kos, the construction of a second strip at Lambi, suitable for night landings by Dakotas, would take some of the pressure off Antimachia. But the Luftwaffe intensified its attacks during the last days of September. On the 27th a Spitfire was damaged at Antimachia. Enemy bombers had flown at an altitude beyond the range of Bofors guns, which had recently been delivered and installed for airfield defence. In the course of the day, 7 (SAAF) Squadron accounted for at least one Bf 109 for three Spitfires shot down. Two Spitfire pilots lost their lives.

The next day, eight reinforcement Spitfire Vs of 74 Squadron arrived from Egypt via Cyprus; a ninth developed engine trouble some 15 miles (24km) off Kastellorizo and was lost, together with the pilot. Spitfires from both squadrons were soon in action, but again it was the hapless South Africans who came off worst when two of their fighters were shot down, resulting in the death of one pilot.

Unlike allied fighters, bombers had the range to reach German targets. Airfields in Crete and Rhodes were attacked during the latter half of September. Both sides were vulnerable to anti-shipping strikes, but the Royal Navy was further disadvantaged in relying on bases far from the scene of operations. This placed an intolerable strain on destroyers, especially Hunt-class vessels, the endurance of which was severely restricted by fuel limitations.

In spite of the difficulties, British forces continued to retain a hold in the Dodecanese. By the beginning of October, 1 DLI had been redeployed, with Battalion Headquarters and A, B, and HQ Companies disposed mainly in bivouac areas extending for a mile from the coast to the north-west outskirts of Platani (Gherme). C Company was allocated Kos town; the Anti-Tank Platoon held the nearby landing ground at Lambi, and Antimachia was left to D Company, two detachments of the Mortar Platoon and one section of the Carrier Platoon.

# Kos, 3 October 1943

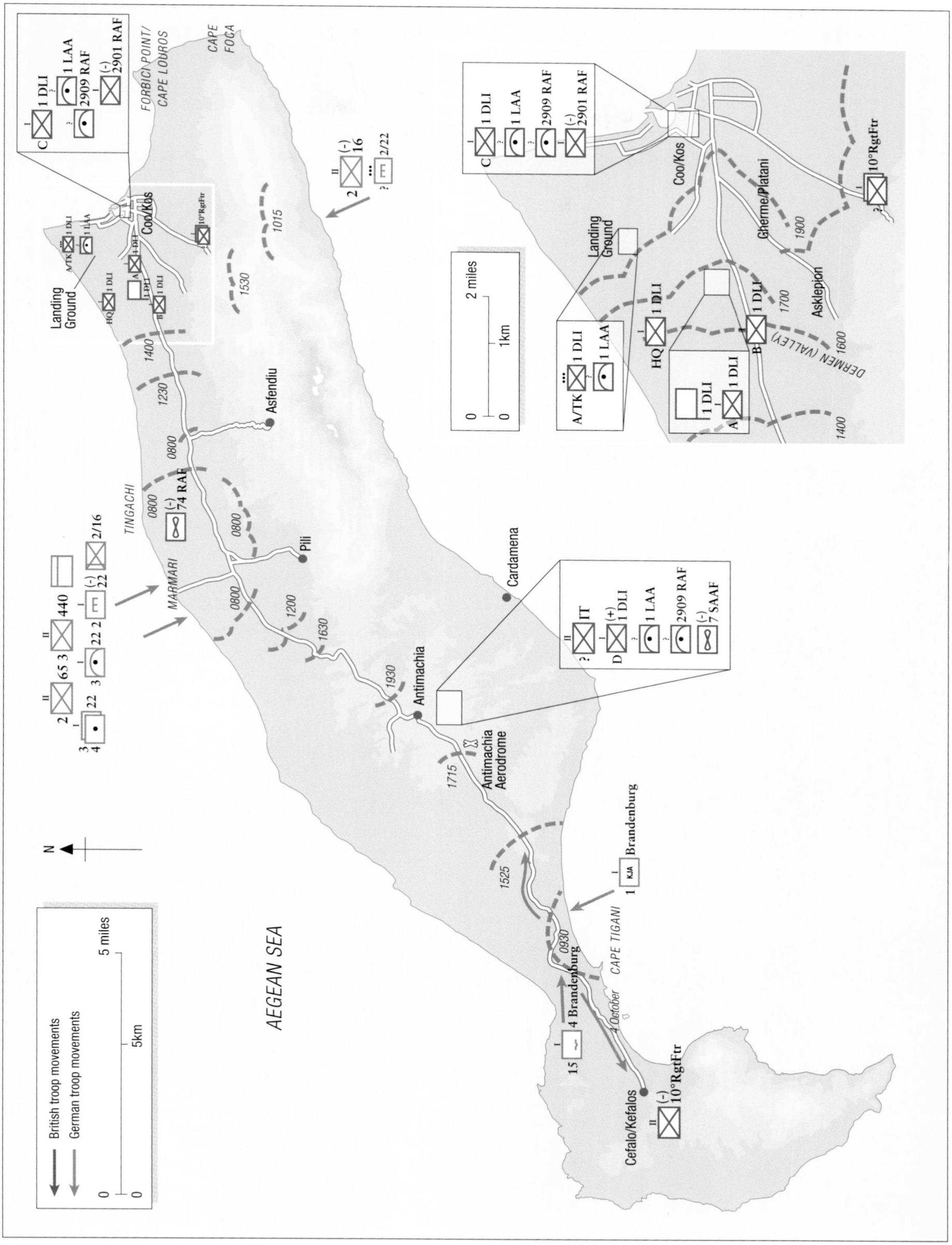

British troop movements
German troop movements
0
5 miles
0
5km
AEGEAN SEA
Cefalo/Kefalos
(-)
10°RgtFtr
15
4 Brandenburg
4 October
CAPE TIGANI
0930
1525
1 KJA Brandenburg
1715
Antimachia Aerodrome
Antimachia
1930
1630
1200
0800
Cardamena
Pili
MARMARI
TINGACHI
(-)
74 RAF
2/16
440
(-)
22
65
22
Asfendiu
1230
1400
1530
1015
2/22
(-)
16
Landing Ground
Coo/Kos
FORBICI POINT/
CAPE LOUROS
CAPE FOCA
C 1 DLI
1 LAA
2909 RAF
(-)
2901 RAF
IT
D (+) 1 DLI
7 SAAF
2 miles
1km
0
A/TK 1 DLI
HQ 1 DLI
B 1 DLI
A 1 DLI
Gherme/Platani
Asklepion
DERMEN (VALLEY)
1900
1700
1600
1400

# OPERATION *EISBÄR*

By Friday morning, 1 October, Generallt. Müller's assault troops had assembled at their departure points. Embarkation was completed that evening and vessels departed to rendezvous the next day in the Cyclades. (On Kos, a German clandestine operation was apparently also under way with the main task of severing main-line communications.) That afternoon, the force divided and set deception courses for Rhodes and Ikaria. Only after dark did the convoy change direction towards Kos. On the 3rd the convoy proceeded to its designated disembarkation points north and south of Kos, unimpeded either by Allied warships or submarines. Operation *Eisbär* was under way.

The first wave of Kampfgruppe von Saldern landed by F-lighter on schedule at 0500hrs. After encountering minimal resistance, II./Gren.Rgt. 65 established a beachhead while F-lighters returned to waiting transports for the next wave.

From just offshore, *UJ 2110* and *UJ 2111* provided fire support and other escort vessels covered the area in smoke. Such was the speed of the German advance that several Spitfires at Tingachi saltpans were captured intact.

The DLI had stood to at 0445hrs as usual, when British Headquarters telephoned to report two unidentified landing craft approaching Marmari. The battalion commander, Lt. Col. Robert Kirby, was in hospital with a knee infection. In his absence the battalion 2 i/c, Maj. Hugh M. Vaux, had taken charge. Vaux readied the counter-attack force (predominantly A and B Companies) and dispatched the Carrier Platoon under Capt. George P. Sivewright on a mobile patrol to the Marmari area. Shortly afterwards, the platoon commander's jeep ran into a burst of machine-gun fire and Sivewright was mortally wounded. Minutes later, an NCO reported to Vaux, confirming that enemy forces had indeed come ashore in the Marmari area and were being engaged by the Carrier Platoon. In the face of superior odds, the Carrier Platoon broke contact and withdrew.

At 0610hrs B Company was ordered to take up a defensive position astride the main road in the Ingirlichi region (west of Platani); HQ Company was

Off Marmari, smokescreens help cover the German landing. The operation, which took place under fire, was nevertheless a complete success. (Author's collection)

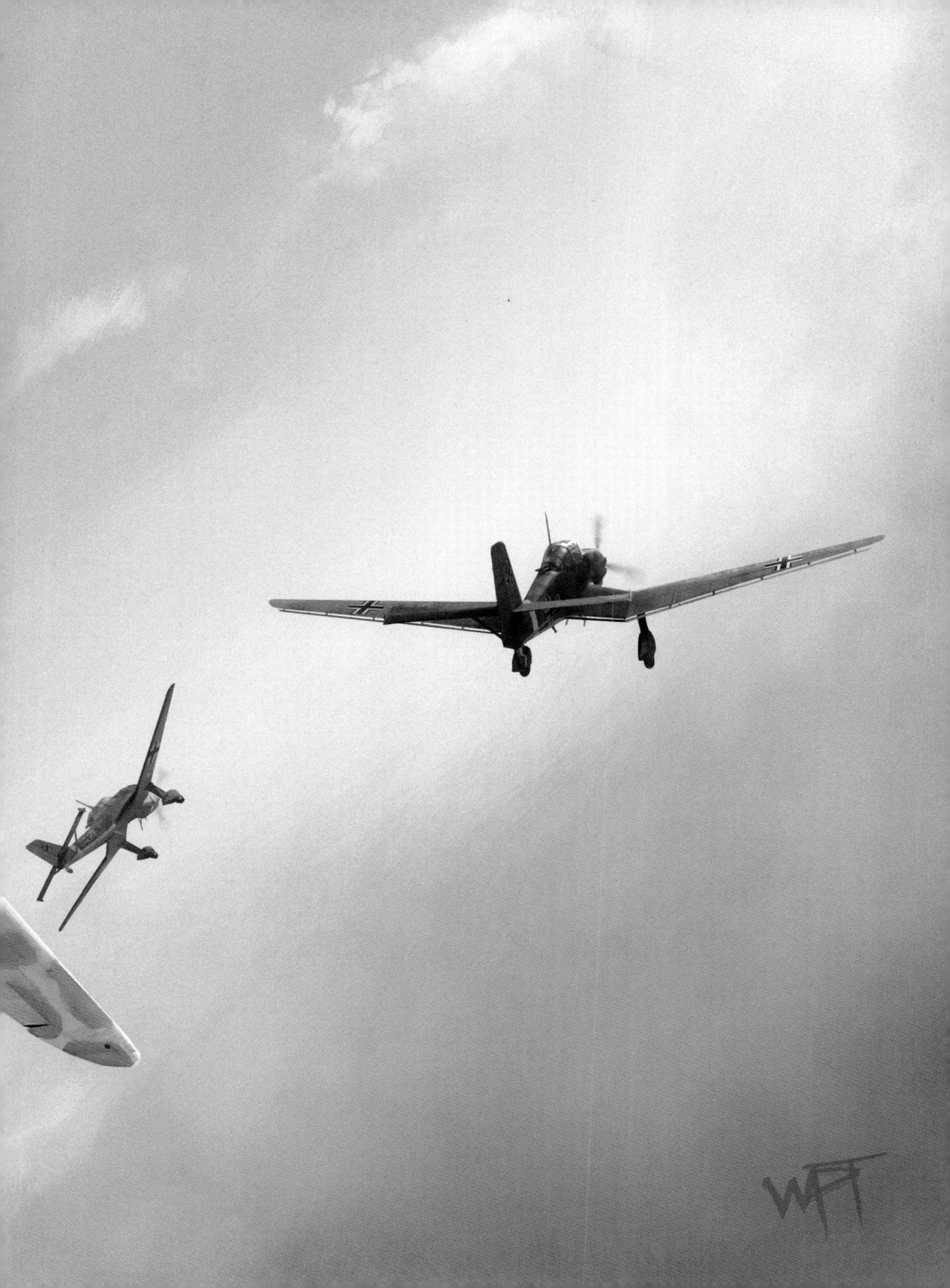

**MAJOR BILL LEVERETTE ATTACKING JU 87 STUKAS, MIDDAY 9 OCTOBER 1943 (PP. 36–37)**

Credential Force was a naval unit comprising the cruiser HMS *Carlisle*, and destroyers HMS *Petard*, *Panther*, and, initially, *Aldenham* and the Greek *Themistocles*, both of which were relieved on Friday, 8 October by HMS *Rockwood* and the Greek *Miaoulis*. On Saturday morning, Credential Force was retiring southward on a course of 160 degrees, some 70 miles north-east of Crete. RAF Beaufighters and American P-38 Lightnings provided air cover. Close to midday, P-38s of 94th FS withdrew shortly before the arrival of a relief flight from 37th FS. At the same time, Ju 87 Stukas of I./St.G. 3 arrived and, facing no aerial opposition, dive-bombed the convoy. HMS *Panther* received a direct hit, split in two and quickly sank. Several bombs struck HMS *Carlisle* aft, rendering her immobile. One Stuka and its crew fell to anti-aircraft fire.

I. Gruppe departed, narrowly avoiding contact with approaching P-38s of 37th FS, led by squadron commander Major Bill Leverette **(1)**. While orbiting the convoy, the P-38 pilots noticed an estimated 25 (II. Gruppe) Stukas en route from the opposite direction. The P-38s changed course to pass behind and above the formation. With three P-38s providing high cover, Leverette's flight of four aircraft dived on the Ju 87s **(2)**.

After he had engaged six Stukas, Leverette closed on a seventh, firing a full burst into the bottom of the fuselage and setting the engine on fire. The Stuka dived abruptly. Leverette was unable to break away upward and in attempting to pass under the right wing, the P-38's left propeller sliced through the enemy machine. The P-38 survived. A running fight continued for some 15 minutes, until the Ju 87s had passed over the south coast of Rhodes. Although some Stukas had struck at the convoy, no ships were lost.

American pilots were credited with destroying 17 enemy aircraft. In addition to Maj. Leverette's seven Ju 87s, five were claimed by Lt. Troy Hanna, three more and a probable by Lt. Homer Sprinkle and one by Lt. Robert Margison. Lieutenant Wayne Blue was credited with a Ju 88 (probably a misidentified 252 Squadron Beaufighter, three of which were attacked by three P-38s). Naval gunners claimed three aircraft shot down. According to Luftwaffe records, seven Ju 87D-3s fell to fighter attack. Another made an emergency landing. One Ju 87D-4 was shot down by AA fire. In all, 12 Luftwaffe aircrew died; 60 naval officers and ratings lost their lives and about 55 were injured.

Among those taken prisoner was the British commander of Kos, Col. Kenyon. Many managed to escape, using whatever means were available. Isolated parties of Allied soldiers and airmen also remained in hiding long after the fighting had ended.

Müller would record that his battle group ultimately took prisoner 3,145 'Badoglio Italians' and 1,388 British. German losses amounted to 14 or 15 dead and at least 70 wounded.

# WAR AT SEA AND ON LAND: 4–11 OCTOBER

On Wednesday, 6 October, IX./Festungsinfanteriebataillon embarked on the steamship *Olympos* and six Marinefährprähme and set sail from Piraeus with *UJ 2111* as escort. The battalion was destined for Kos, to take over from the combat units there, enabling them to prepare for the forthcoming invasion of Leros. Early the next day, the British submarine *Unruly* sighted the convoy off Kos. After an unsuccessful torpedo attack, *Unruly* surfaced and opened fire with her deck gun. *Olympos* was struck and veered away and an F-lighter was set on fire and immobilized before the escort vessel also began taking hits. *UJ 2111* was saved by the appearance of four aircraft. *Unruly* broke off the attack and dived, following which the escort vessel and five of the six F-lighters continued at speed towards Kos.

Meanwhile, the Royal Navy cruisers *Sirius* and *Penelope* in company with the destroyers *Faulknor* and *Fury* were racing towards the scene. The destroyers intercepted and sunk *Olympos* and rejoined the cruisers in attacking the rest of the convoy. *UJ 2111* was so severely damaged that she had to be abandoned by her crew. The warships then turned their fire on survivors in the water. After withdrawing, the British warships were targeted by German aircraft, resulting in substantial losses in dead and wounded.

At least one German vessel, a badly damaged landing craft, was able to reach Astipalaea. On board were 80 or more personnel, soon to become prisoners of the island's resident Italian forces and M2 Patrol of the LRDG.

On 8 October, *Unruly* went on to torpedo and sink a minelayer south of Amorgos. *Bulgaria*, with a crew of 81, had also been bound for Kos, with 285 men of X./Festungsinfanteriebataillon (in all, 300 were rescued).

While the Royal Navy engaged enemy forces at sea, minor actions were taking place on some islands. On 4 October a composite patrol (X1) of the LRDG under New Zealander Capt R. A. Tinker had been evacuated by caique after several days on Pserimos. All but one man, who was presumed captured, reached nearby Kalymnos in time for a general withdrawal to Leros that night. The Italian garrison surrendered without a fight, whereupon the island was taken over by III./Gren.Rgt. 440 and Küstenjägerkompanie 'Brandenburg'.

Elsewhere, some 26 men of the Special Boat Squadron under Capt. 'Jock' Lapraik had turned Symi into a base from which to infiltrate enemy-held islands. The SBS were joined by a six-man LRDG patrol led by Capt. Alan Redfern, and unexpectedly reinforced on 3 October by 40 ground crew of 74 Squadron, who arrived while en route to join their unit on Kos, unaware that the island was practically already under German control. An Italian garrison of approximately 140 completed the mixed force. Early on Thursday morning, 7 October, a large caique was allowed to enter Pedi Bay. By the time the mistake was realized, German troops and a small number of Italian Fascists had already disembarked. The force – about 90 strong – reached the outskirts of Symi town (Yalos/Chorio) before the advance faltered. There was fighting until mid-afternoon, when three Ju 87 Stukas arrived and carried out a diversionary raid, enabling survivors of the Axis force to withdraw. Six prisoners and 16 confirmed dead were left behind. One SBS man had also been killed, together with a number of civilians. Air raids continued the next day, resulting in further casualties. On the 11th, the little town of Symi was bombed again and all but destroyed, prompting the evacuation of British forces from the island.

In the meantime, American fighters made a rare appearance over the Aegean. On 8 October, the cruiser HMS *Carlisle* was southbound with four destroyers: the Greek *Miaoulis* and HM ships *Panther*, *Petard* and *Rockwood*. At 0750hrs on Saturday, 9 October, two low-flying Arados were sighted, evidently shadowing the warships. One aircraft was claimed damaged and the other driven off by a patrolling Beaufighter. The convoy continued unescorted until the arrival 40 minutes later of a number of American Lockheed P-38 Lightnings. Thereafter, air cover was provided for the rest of the morning, each formation remaining until the arrival of its relief flight. Beaufighters continued to provide additional protection.

Towards midday, several minutes elapsed during which there was no air cover and, as fate would have it, there now appeared Ju 87s of I./Sturzkampfgeschwader 3 (I./St.G. 3). One Stuka after another dived onto its chosen target. They were met with a tremendous barrage by the ships' guns, but at 1202hrs, bombs struck HMS *Carlisle* aft, dealing a crippling blow. HMS *Panther* also received a direct hit, broke in two and sank soon afterwards.

The I./St.G. 3 aircraft departed, narrowly avoiding contact with seven approaching Lightnings of 37th Fighter Squadron, led by Maj. W. L. (Bill) Leverette. No sooner had the American aircraft reached the convoy than three formations of Ju 87s were observed approaching from the north-west.

II./St.G. 3, arriving at the worst possible time, was about to pay for the successful attack of I. Gruppe. The slower Stukas were no match for the Lightnings. Seven were shot down, together with a Ju 88.

HMS *Carlisle* was taken in tow by *Rockwood* and brought back to Alexandria, but the damage was such that she would never again put to sea. Such costly efforts by the British only served to delay the inevitable. The situation might have been very different if the Americans had agreed to extend their air support for, in addition to providing cover for the Royal Navy, Lightnings also carried out shipping sweeps and strafing attacks and bombing raids against Kos. Instead, just as they were making their presence felt, the Lightning squadrons were recalled. Without effective air cover, how could British forces retain a hold in the Dodecanese?

# WAR AT SEA: 12–21 OCTOBER

On 12 October, the British ML 835 (motor launch) was written off during an air raid at Leros. Five days later, the cruiser HMS *Sirius* was damaged and nearly 50 of her crew were killed or wounded in an attack by Ju 88s. At about this time, HM submarine *Trooper* disappeared east of Leros, probably after striking a mine. And on the 21st, heavy seas accounted for the British ML 1015.

In spite of such losses, British and Greek naval units remained a potent force. Off Kinaros on 16 October, HM submarine *Torbay* sunk the steamship *Kari*, with 500 troops on board (by 18 October 320 survivors had been rescued). At Kalymnos, during the night of 16–17 October, *UJ 2109* (formerly HMS *Widnes*) was attacked and written off, the merchantman *Trapani* was set on fire and *F 338* burnt out aft as a result of attacks by HMS *Hursley* and the Greek *Miaoulis*; a steamship, *Santorini*, was badly damaged, probably by the same destroyers. Shipping strikes by the Royal Air Force also produced results. Off the north coast of Kos on the night of 18–19 October, motor torpedo boats attacked the German patrol boat *LS 5* and landing craft *F 131*, destroying the latter. North of Kos port, another

Shipping was especially vulnerable to air attack. East of Karpathos on 9 October, Ju 87s of I./St.G. 3 struck at a joint British-Greek naval convoy. The destroyer HMS *Panther* was sunk and the cruiser HMS *Carlisle* (pictured) was hit aft and taken under tow to Alexandria. Such was the damage that she would never put to sea again. (Author's collection)

American pilots of 37th Fighter Squadron following the successful aerial actions of 9 October 1943. From left, Thomas W. 'Dub' Smith, Lt. Homer L. Sprinkle (killed in a flying accident on 18 October), Lt. Harry T. Hanna, Lt. Wayne L. Blue, Maj. William L. 'Speedy' Leverette, Lt. Robert L. Margison, Lt. Elmer H. La Rue (missing in action 16 January 1944). (Roger Leverette)

German landing craft, *F 330*, was burnt out after onboard ammunition detonated, and on or about the 19th, Allied aircraft sunk the German coast patrol boat *GK 51*.

During the night of 18–19 October, Wellingtons of 38 Squadron torpedoed and sank the merchantman *Sinfra*. On board were 204 German troops, 2,389 Italian and 71 Greek prisoners. It was not the only such tragedy. According to the Kriegsmarine, by 22 October, 6,000 mainly Italian prisoners had perished as a consequence of transport vessels being lost through Allied action.

## LEVITHA

A series of events was also taking place that was to impact on the future of the Long Range Desert Group. By 24 September, within days of occupying Astipalaea, held by a garrison of several hundred Italians, three LRDG patrols had returned to Leros, leaving only M2 Patrol under Capt. Ken Lazarus to report on enemy aircraft and shipping movements.

On Thursday, 14 October, the trawler *Hedgehog* of the Levant Schooner Flotilla sailed from Leros with supplies for M2 Patrol. The commander, Sub-Lt. David N. Harding, RNVR, was to return with survivors of the ill-fated *Olympos* convoy who were still being held captive on Astipalaea. In all, more than 50 German prisoners were embarked.

Soon after 0600hrs on 16 October, HM submarine *Surf* encountered *Hedgehog* and, as her engine had ceased, took her in tow towards Levitha. When a low-flying enemy aircraft appeared, *Surf* slipped the tow and dived. On resurfacing, it was seen that *Hedgehog* was again operating under her own steam and she was left to proceed unaided.

*Hedgehog* reached Levitha. Exactly what happened next is unclear, but at some point, the German prisoners took control and reported the situation, probably via the island's Italian wireless link. *Hedgehog* was written off after being burnt out in undisclosed circumstances.

On Sunday evening, 17 October, Oblt. Oschatz commanding 15./4. Rgt. 'Brandenburg' was tasked with part of his company to seize Levitha and rescue their fellow countrymen. Early the next morning, the assault force was airlifted from Athens-Phaleron in two Ju 52 seaplanes and a Dornier flyingboat, with three Arados as escort and three more providing forward reconnaissance. According to plan, the transport aircraft alighted just off Levitha, and the troops prepared rubber dinghies for the short trip ashore. As it was being released from the Dornier one of the inflatables capsized and an occupant was dragged under water by the weight of ammunition boxes and equipment. After resurfacing two or three times, the unfortunate paratrooper disappeared altogether. He would be the only German fatality of the operation.

The landing and subsequent sweep through the island was unopposed. But two Italians were fatally wounded at a wireless station when it was shot up and bombed by Arados. Contact was established with the *Olympos* survivors and by 1330hrs, just four and a half hours after their arrival, the paratroopers had secured the island. Sub-Lieutenant Harding and his crew were prisoners, together with 11 Italians who had been stationed on the island. That afternoon, most of the assault unit departed after being relieved by troops of 11. Kompanie of III./Luftwaffen-Jägerregiment 21 (11./Lw.-Jg. Rgt. 21). The remaining Brandenburger left by Ju 52 the next day.

On 22 October, just three days after its last troops had been evacuated from Levitha, 15./4. Rgt. 'Brandenburg' made a parachute drop on Astipalaea in conjunction with air-sea landings by 1./1. Regiment 'Brandenburg', the latter arriving in seaplanes and paddling to shore in rubber dinghies.

As a preliminary to the invasion, the Luftwaffe targeted key installations, destroying an Italian wireless station at Porto Scala. As they advanced, the Germans freed 48 German prisoners, most if not all of them survivors of the *Olympos* convoy. The Italians put up minimal resistance, so that by 1400hrs the Germans were already in control of the island. Among those taken prisoner were a number of LRDG. For this small select force, events were about to become even worse.

The next day, a Fascist radio broadcast reported that Axis prisoners of war on Levitha had overpowered their captors. The commander of 234 Brigade on Leros, newly promoted Maj. Gen. Brittorous, ordered that Levitha be retaken. Those selected for the task were nearly all LRDG. Specialists whose role was primarily to gather intelligence and to undertake deep penetration mobile patrols now underwent hurried training to familiarize themselves with collapsible assault boats (folboats).

That same evening, ML 579 and ML 836 embarked 24 and 25 troops respectively and set out from Leros. 'Olforce' was equipped and organized along infantry lines into two sections,

An unusual role for paratroopers, as 15./4.Rgt. 'Brandenburg' disembark from Ju 52 floatplanes just off the coast of Levitha, before paddling to shore in rubber dinghies. (BA: 101I-525-2290-15)

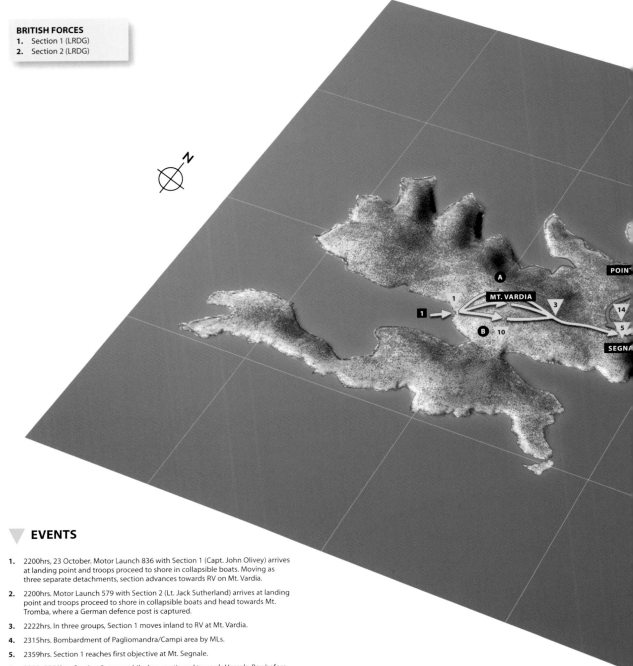

**BRITISH FORCES**
1. Section 1 (LRDG)
2. Section 2 (LRDG)

## ▼ EVENTS

1. 2200hrs, 23 October. Motor Launch 836 with Section 1 (Capt. John Olivey) arrives at landing point and troops proceed to shore in collapsible boats. Moving as three separate detachments, section advances towards RV on Mt. Vardia.

2. 2200hrs. Motor Launch 579 with Section 2 (Lt. Jack Sutherland) arrives at landing point and troops proceed to shore in collapsible boats and head towards Mt. Tromba, where a German defence post is captured.

3. 2222hrs. In three groups, Section 1 moves inland to RV at Mt. Vardia.

4. 2315hrs. Bombardment of Pagliomandra/Campi area by MLs.

5. 2359hrs. Section 1 reaches first objective at Mt. Segnale.

6. 2200–2359hrs. Section 2, meanwhile, has continued towards Vurcalo Bay before changing direction south and seizing high ground at Mt. Calasuria, along with a number of German prisoners.

7. 0300hrs, 24 October. Detachments 1 (Cpl. Tom Bradfield) and 2 (Cpl. Harris) sent to Point 106 with orders to work along ridge, east to Point 81.

8. 0530hrs. Bren gun team (two men) are captured while attempting to take up position in area of Castello feature.

9. 0700–1100hrs. At about 0700hrs, Detachment 3 (Gnr. Jim Patch) is sent to relieve detachments on Point 106.

10. At about 0930hrs, a party from Detachment 1 sent to fetch ammunition stockpiled at Mt. Vardia return with three German prisoners.

11. Later in the morning, all three detachments are tasked with dislodging enemy forces from the Castello feature.

12. 1215hrs. German forces are observed in the area of Pagliomandra, apparently gathering for an attack.

13. 1245hrs. German troops are observed in the south-eastern part of the island. Detachments 1, 2 and 3 are pinned down between Point 106 and the Castello feature. Over the next few hours, the high ground of Mts Piriallo, Calasuria and Tromba are overrun by three infantry groups, with Stukas and Arados providing air support.

14. 1515hrs. German four-man team carry out a surprise attack on Section 1 HQ at Mt. Segnale. Capt. Olivey and one OR escape.

15. The majority of Section 2, in the eastern part of Levitha, surrender at about 1630–1700hrs. A few who evade capture are taken prisoner some days later. Later that night, seven of the original 49 LRDG are evacuated by motor launch.

# LEVITHA, 23–24 OCTOBER 1943

LRDG landing and advance inland and German counterattack

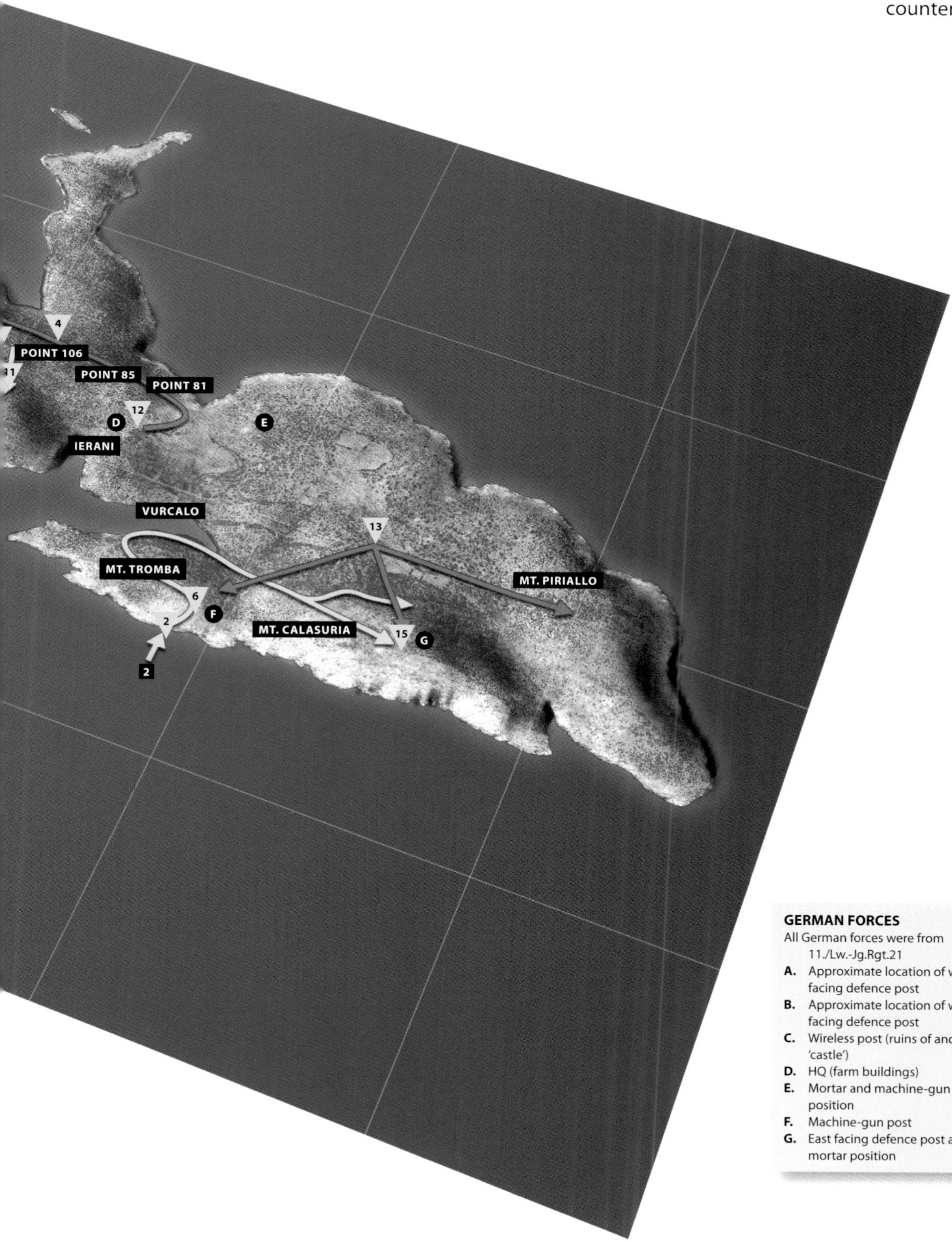

4
POINT 106
POINT 85
POINT 81
12
D
E
IERANI
VURCALO
13
MT. TROMBA
MT. PIRIALLO
6
F
2
MT. CALASURIA
15
G
2


**GERMAN FORCES**

All German forces were from 11./Lw.-Jg.Rgt.21

- **A.** Approximate location of west facing defence post
- **B.** Approximate location of west facing defence post
- **C.** Wireless post (ruins of ancient 'castle')
- **D.** HQ (farm buildings)
- **E.** Mortar and machine-gun position
- **F.** Machine-gun post
- **G.** East facing defence post and mortar position

each comprising three detachments and a headquarters, with Capt. John R. Olivey in overall command and OC Section 1, and with Lt. Jack Sutherland OC Section 2. Also with Section 1 were Capt. Dick Lawson (medical officer) and an attached officer from The Border Regiment, Lt. John H. Kay.

The main joint objective was high central ground, which overlooked the southern port of Levitha and from where it was proposed to deny the rest of the island to enemy forces (a detachment of 11./Lw.-Jg.Rgt. 21). Section 1 was to land in the western Baia del Fico, and Section 2 near Cape Tromba on the south coast. Once ashore, each section was expected to establish its own headquarters and clear the surrounding area. At dawn, the two sections were to link up while retaining any commanding positions occupied during the night. At 2200hrs the MLs would return and, depending on the situation, either offload stores or disembark an Italian garrison force. In the event of failure, both sections were to make for the western end of the island to await evacuation.

The voyage from Leros took nearly three hours. On reaching Levitha, the folboats were launched and, loaded with men and equipment, steered towards shore. Neither landing was opposed, but as per operation instructions, the MLs engaged likely shore targets before they withdrew (a move that only alerted enemy forces).

The first prominent height along Olivey's route was Point 133 (Mount Vardia), where the section's 2-inch mortar, extra ammunition and stores were cached. In the dark, the section unknowingly bypassed defensive posts on either side of the feature, continuing unchallenged towards nearby Point 130 (Segnale). Headquarters was set up on a plateau on the summit where prepared defence works surrounded unoccupied Italian buildings. Farther east, Sutherland's party was already in action, one New Zealander being severely injured by an exploding grenade.

Having avoided detection, Olivey decided to seize their next objective before dawn and ahead of schedule. Two patrols under Sgt. Harris and Cpl. Thomas Bradfield were tasked with proceeding and linking up with

During the Brandenburg operation, two Italians lost their lives and one German paratrooper was drowned. In turn, some 50 former prisoners of war were rescued and their erstwhile captors, the crew of *Hedgehog* (Levant Schooner Flotilla), taken prisoner. Four of the crew are seen under guard. The man on the right is thought to be Stoker John Wallace, from Belfast. (BA: 101I-525-2291-08A)

Sutherland's section. By first light both detachments had reached a ridgeline in the centre of the island (Pagliomandra). They then came under rifle and machine-gun fire from the vicinity of an ancient stone ruin on Point 112 (Castello). Bradfield was withdrawn to Segnale with a serious arm wound, following which Olivey recalled the patrols. At about the same time on Castello, a Bren gun team was taken prisoner while moving into position to provide covering fire.

Meanwhile, Sutherland's section had attacked German positions in the south-east of the island, seizing a machine gun on Point 74 (Mount Tromba) and a mortar on Point 141 (Mount Calasuria). When a second New Zealander was seriously wounded, Tpr. W. R. (Ron) Hill assisted the medical orderly in finding cover for the casualty. In doing so he came upon what he thought was a cleared German position. It was, however, still occupied. After a very brief action, nine Germans surrendered. By daybreak, the high ground was secured, and some 35 prisoners had been taken.

With daylight, the situation began to deteriorate. Having lost the initiative, the LRDG found itself targeted by German machine-gunners and, worse, aircraft. Morale received a much-needed boost when an Arado seaplane made a forced landing several miles offshore after being shot up by both sections. A while later, two Rhodesian soldiers returned from Mount Vardia, where they had been sent by Olivey to fetch the section 2-inch mortar and to bring up extra ammunition. They also brought with them three prisoners. (The prisoners were later evacuated to the western slope of Segnale but escaped after overpowering one of their two guards; the other guard fled.)

Late in the morning, the three detachments were re-deployed in an unsuccessful effort to eject enemy forces from Castello. During the day, two men in Section 2 were detailed to fetch water from where it had been cached with their boats, and to report on the situation in the area. They took along a German prisoner. Neither of the LRDG pair was seen again. Their fate and that of the German prisoner of war is unknown.

At about 1515hrs, Olivey on the east side of Point 130 was surprised to hear a familiar voice calling for him to surrender. Seeing Lt. Kay, escorted by two German soldiers, Olivey drew his revolver and opened fire before fleeing with Rhodesian Gnr. Rupping. The LRDG on Segnale had been taken totally by surprise, outmanoeuvred by just four men. German reinforcements arrived, who then proceeded to ambush and capture a returning LRDG patrol.

Section 2 had been prevented from advancing farther owing to ongoing air attacks. The way forward was also swept by German machine guns. Mortar fire aggravated the situation. During mid-afternoon Stukas provided air cover for approaching German troops.

As dusk approached, and with German forces closing in, Sutherland's men were dispersed between three locations: Headquarters was on relatively low ground close to the landing place in the area of Mount Tromba; Sgt. Dobson's party was situated centrally,

On 22 October, within days of its successful Levitha operation, 15./4.Rgt. 'Brandenburg' mounted a parachute assault against Astipalaea in conjunction with an air-sea landing by 1./1.Rgt. 'Brandenburg'. Among those taken prisoner were a number of LRDG personnel. (BA: 101I-526-2301-16A)

and a few men under Cpl. Gill were holding out on nearby high ground. Section 2 was using captured weapons after running out of ammunition, fighting with backs to the sea, and outnumbered by the enemy. With little other option, Sutherland surrendered.

Of the LRDG, five had been killed or were reported missing. Thirty-seven were taken prisoner. It was the worst single disaster to have befallen the force. Only Olivey, Rupping and five other members of Section 1 evaded capture to be evacuated by motor launch.

## WAR AT SEA: 22–31 OCTOBER

In the meantime, off Kalymnos, many lives had been lost during the night of 22–23 October, when mines sank HMS *Hurworth* and blew away the forecastle of the Greek destroyer *Adrias* (she eventually reached the safe port of Alexandria). In the early hours of the 24th, the same minefield claimed HMS *Eclipse*. Fatalities included well over 100 army personnel, mainly 4 Buffs en route to Leros. The same day, the Italian merchantman SS *Taganrog* was bombed and sunk and, on the 26th, ML 579 was destroyed and four of her crew killed in an air raid at Arki. Two days later, LCT 115 (Landing Craft Tank) together with 22 men and four heavy anti-aircraft guns was lost to air attack some 35 miles (56km) off Kastellorizo. Well over 60 of her crew were killed and wounded when HMS *Aurora* was severely damaged in an air attack on the 30th; another destroyer, HMS *Belvoir*, had a lucky escape when a bomb that struck her failed to explode. And at Samos, the Italian ex-trawler *Morrhua* was bombed and sunk. During the same period, the Royal Navy had some success when HM submarine *Unsparing* torpedoed the German troopship *Ingeborg* and later sank a rescue vessel, Nioi.

## CHANGE OF COMMAND AT LEROS

Initially, on Leros, a combined Naval and Brigade Headquarters was established at Lakki. As bombing of the port intensified, Brigade Headquarters shifted to San Nicola, to be followed by Naval Headquarters two days later on 6 October. When bombs began to fall dangerously close to San Nicola, Mt Meraviglia, in central Leros, was selected as a more suitable location for what became known as Fortress Headquarters. However, during daylight hours, when the Luftwaffe was active, the brigade commander preferred another, less hazardous, spot near Partheni. This did not pass unnoticed and undoubtedly contributed to the departure of Brittorous just days before the expected German invasion of Leros.

On 1 November, Maj. Gen. Hall was appointed General Officer Commanding Aegean. On 5 November, Hall and Brig. Tilney arrived on Leros, and Headquarters Aegean assumed control of operations. Hall would make Samos his headquarters and departed on 11 November, leaving on Leros Tilney, who relieved Brittorous as Fortress Commander.

When Tilney took over his predecessor's command centre, he was not impressed. Conditions at Fortress Headquarters were less than ideal. Men and equipment were crammed inside a tunnel that ran through the hilltop, with an entrance at each end and a vertical shaft providing access to an observation post. As Tilney would soon discover, communications were to present a serious problem owing to insufficient and inadequate equipment and terrain that allowed only restricted wireless links at the best of times.

# WAR AT SEA AND IN THE AIR: 1–11 NOVEMBER

In the first days of November, Allied aircraft searched for shipping assembling for the expected German assault on Leros. But daylight moves between staging points were protected by fighters, and at night dispersed vessels were virtually impossible to detect. For Allied aircrews, every sortie was a risk. On 5 November alone, Beaufighter units lost six aircraft and four crews: Bf 109s of 8./J.G. 27 accounted for four machines of 227 Squadron on an offensive sweep around Rhodes and, at Lavrion Bay off the Greek mainland, two crews of 47 Squadron were taken prisoner when their aircraft were shot down by ship's flak. On the 6th a low-level shipping strike left the German *R 34* and *R 194* disabled. At least three were killed and many more wounded. 603 Squadron lost one aircraft and 47 Squadron lost two machines (together with one crew), while another aircraft belly-landed on returning to Gambut (two pilots of 7./J.G. 27 were each credited with a Beaufighter destroyed). On the 7th, a Beaufighter of 252 Squadron was written off and the crew injured in a take-off accident. Three days later, a pilot in 47 Squadron was killed and a 603 Squadron crew taken prisoner when two more Beaufighters fell to Messerschmitts of III./J.G. 27.

As well as shipping strikes, Allied aircrew flew reconnaissance missions, carried out mine-laying operations and made night-bombing raids on Antimachia airfield. But it was not enough to prevent the Luftwaffe from maintaining air superiority, or to lessen the threat German aircraft posed to Allied warships.

Seen from Meraviglia shortly after the end of the battle for Leros: an excellent view of Leros town (now Platanos) overlooked by the island's medieval castle on Point 189. During the battle, a platoon of the Royal Irish Fusiliers held out at the castle until 15 November. (Author's collection)

On the night of 10–11 November, Allied warships targeted German invasion craft assembling for the expected invasion of Leros. The British destroyers *Petard* and *Rockwood* and the Polish *Krakowiak* bombarded Kalymnos harbour, where escort vessels sustained splinter damage; *Trapani*, damaged in a previous attack, was set on fire and capsized. While withdrawing, HMS *Rockwood* was struck by a glide bomb that, luckily, failed to explode. HM ships *Faulknor*, *Beaufort* and the Greek *Pindos* also bombarded Kos harbour, albeit with little effect.

Hardly any images have emerged showing Allied forces on Kos or Leros. This rare photograph taken atop Scumbarda shows New Zealander Second Lieutenant Frank White (second from right) with members of his LRDG callsign, apparently observing aerial activity above their position. (Brendan O'Carroll)

## ENIGMA AND *ULTRA*

Winston Churchill was kept well informed with regard to German intentions, knowing in advance such crucial details as enemy shipping movements. Since the beginning of hostilities, the Germans had relied on Enigma, a machine designed for the encryption and decryption of secret messages. But transmissions were being intercepted and passed on to cryptanalysts and translators at Bletchley Park in Buckinghamshire, England. When, during the night of 6–7 November, a German signaller advised that the code word 'Leopard' had been replaced with '*Taifun*', it was duly noted by British Intelligence and passed on to the British prime minister. '*Ultra*', as the decoding operation was called, had to remain a closely guarded secret. Being seen to act on information that could have derived only from Enigma would also inform the Germans that their supposedly indecipherable means of communication had been compromised.

On 11 November, air reconnaissance observed considerable movement of landing craft between Kos and Kalymnos. It was also known through *Ultra* that *Taifun* was to commence the following day. However, British relief destroyers were not expected to arrive in the area of operations until late on 12–13 November, making it essential for those already there to conserve fuel. HMS *Faulknor* and two Hunt-class destroyers were therefore diverted to an anchorage near the Kos Channel, from where the Hunts could be sent to attack any landing craft that might be reported off Kos. The force arrived at Alakishli Bay in the early hours of Friday, 12 November, by which time Operation *Taifun* was already under way.

## OPERATION *TAIFUN*: 12 NOVEMBER

Embarkation of German forces destined for Leros had been completed by about 2000hrs on Thursday, 11 November. Meanwhile, some two to three miles (3–5km) off Leros, BYMS 72 (British Yard Minesweeper) was on a supply run to the island, when she was attacked by Dornier Do 217s and struck by a remote-controlled Henschel Hs 293 glide bomb. The explosion brought down the ship's mast, knocked out the port Oerlikon and damaged the

# Leros, 12 November 1943

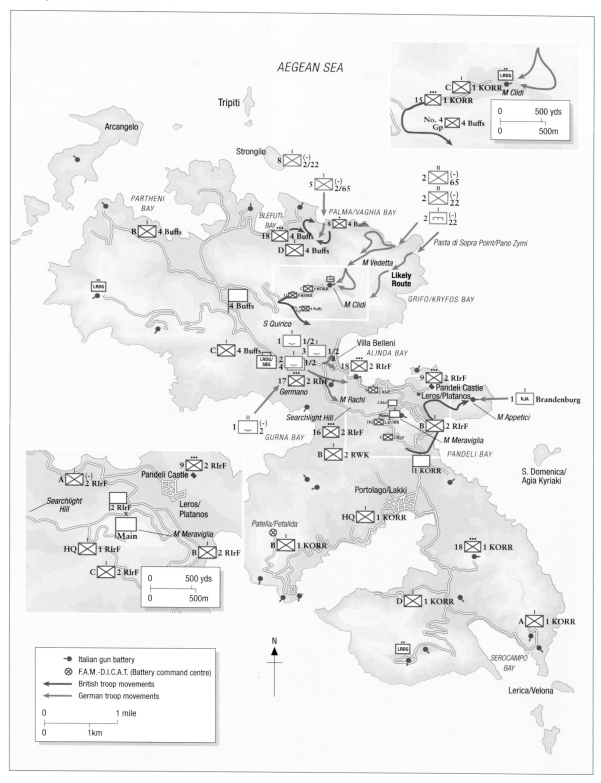

AEGEAN SEA

Tripiti

Arcangelo

PARTHENI BAY

Strongilo

BLEFUTI BAY

PALMA/VAGHIA BAY

Pasta di Sopra Point/Pano Zymi

M Vedetta

**Likely Route**

M Clidi

GRIFO/KRYFOS BAY

S Quirico

Villa Belleni

ALINDA BAY

Germano

M Rachi

Searchlight Hill

GURNA BAY

Pandeli Castle
Leros/Platanos

Brandenburg

M Appetici

M Meraviglia

PANDELI BAY

S. Domenica/
Agia Kyriaki

Portolago/Lakki

Patella/Petalida

Searchlight Hill

Pandeli Castle

Leros/Platanos

Main

M Meraviglia

SEROCAMPO BAY

Lerica/Velona

0          500 yds
0          500m

N

Legend:
- Italian gun battery
- ⊗ F.A.M.-D.I.C.A.T. (Battery command centre)
- British troop movements
- German troop movements

0          1 mile
0          1km

0          500 yds
0          500m

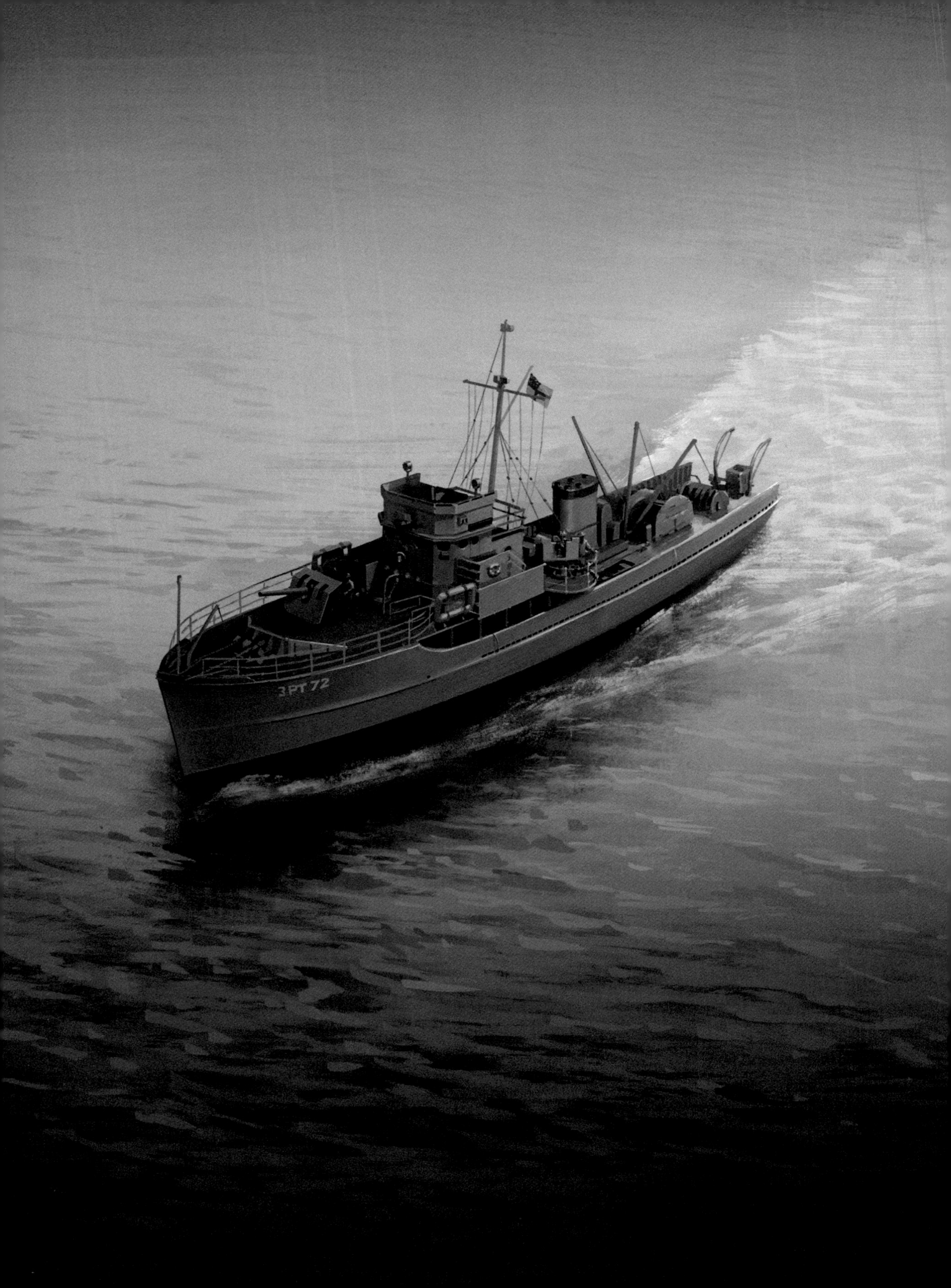
3 PT 72

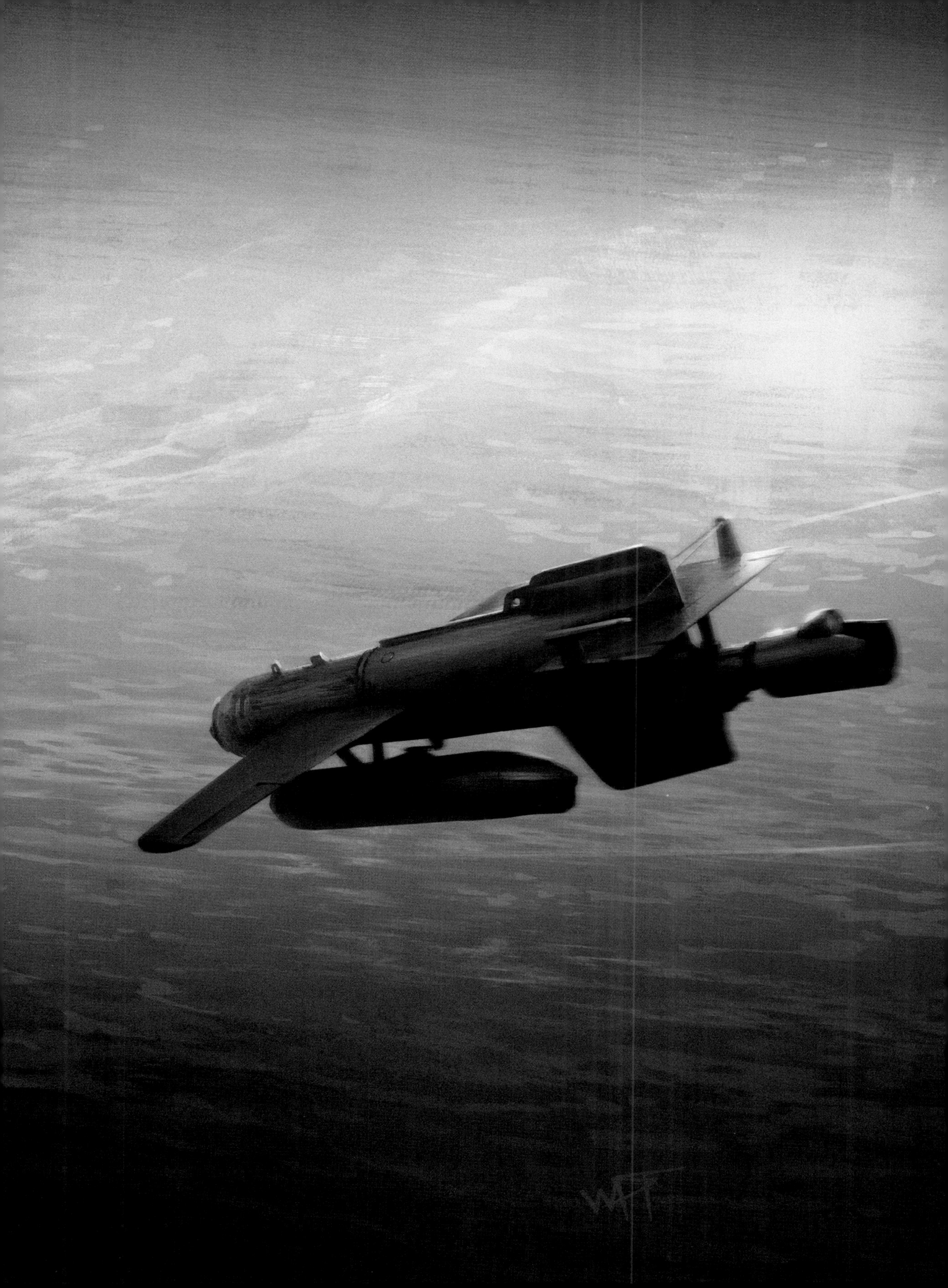

**BYMS 72: GLIDE BOMB ATTACK, NIGHT 11/12 NOVEMBER 1943 (PP. 52–53)**

The British Yard Minesweeper was an American-built wooden vessel, supplied to Britain for the Royal Navy. J872 was launched at New York on 7 April 1943. The hull number was eventually changed to 3PT72, although the ship is more often referred to as BYMS 72 **(1)**. In August 1943, she passed through the Straits of Gibraltar and into the Mediterranean. On 8 November, BYMS 72 together with 73 began operations in the Aegean, transporting troops and supplies to Leros. During the night of 10–11 November, both ships left Kastellorizo with reinforcements and supplies. BYMS 72 could not be offloaded in sufficient time, however, and departed Leros still carrying essential stores. The minesweeper returned the next night but was attacked some two to three miles from the island. Due to the noise of the ship's engines, those on board did not hear the approaching danger. Although it was a full moon, neither was anything seen. At least one aircraft, probably a Dornier Do 217, carried a Henschel Hs 293 glide bomb **(2)**. The 'glide bomb' was actually a jet-propelled radio-controlled missile with a 600lb explosive warhead. A red tail tracer unit assisted the operator in following the missile's course

from his position in the launch aircraft. Although limited in the number of steering movements, the operator had no difficulty zeroing in on his target. On board the BYMS, a crewman shouted a warning. Possibly, he had noticed the glow from the tail unit. Moments later, the minesweeper was struck amidships in the area of the portside Oerlikon **(3)**, resulting in the deaths of at least two men and wounding others. The minesweeper then came under machine-gun fire. Before long, two small craft put out from Leros and the badly damaged BYMS was assisted into Alinda Bay, where dead and injured were taken ashore. The vessel was then directed to the main port at Lakki. She never arrived, missing the entrance in the dark and continuing in the direction of Kalymnos. Unfortunately, BYMS 72 then encountered ships of the German western landing group, meeting with such a concentration of automatic fire that no one on board could react. The minesweeper was captured. As a result of both attacks, six were killed or would die of their injuries. Three men escaped by swimming to Kalymnos. At least 16 of the crew were taken prisoner. The eventual fate of the vessel is unknown.

steering, leaving BYMS 72 circling helplessly. Two men were killed, five were injured and one was missing. ML 299 and MTB 315 (motor torpedo boat) put out from Leros to assist. Travelling on the latter was Lt. Cdr. L. F. (Frank) Ramseyer. He boarded the minesweeper and assumed control and, with the steering gear temporarily repaired, managed to pilot her into Alinda Bay.

That night, at Kalymnos, the invasion convoy had just got under way when two destroyers were sighted. Their identity could not be ascertained (in fact, they were almost certainly German), but as an hour's contingency had been included in the planning of *Taifun*, time was allowed for the destroyers to clear the area; Y-Time was to remain unchanged. Accordingly, the Kos convoy departed at 2300hrs with *R 195* leading the way.

Later still, the Kos flotilla was sighted and bombed by Wellingtons, albeit without effect. It was assumed that the vessels were assembling preparatory to a daylight landing. Even so, the threat posed by mines precluded a pre-emptive strike by the Royal Navy. That this was in fact the main (eastern) force actually en route to Leros was not appreciated until it was far too late. It has been since argued that even if the navy had acted, the enemy would have received sufficient warning to avoid an attack and to respond with retaliatory action. The only certainty is that the opportunity to strike had now passed. The Kos flotilla reached the rendezvous at Kalolimnos and was joined by the delayed force from Kalymnos about an hour later. Both units then proceeded on course for Leros.

After unloading the dead and injured at Alinda, BYMS 72 was again also under way, having been ordered to Lakki for immediate repairs. But in the dark, the vessel steamed past the harbour entrance and continued towards Kalymnos. She was intercepted by the German *R 210* and hailed in English by the captain, Oblt. z.S. Hansjürgen Weissenborn. He guided the minesweeper towards *UJ 2101* and *UJ 2102*, whereupon the BYMS was subjected to a joint attack. Three of the crew were killed and several wounded, including the commanding officer and First Lieutenant. Both officers, together with 14 ratings, were taken prisoner. Three ratings were able to swim to safety. The minesweeper, apparently with codebooks intact, was taken under tow and beached at Kalymnos.

Shortly before 0500hrs, ML 456 encountered the eastern invasion force 12 miles (20km) east of Leros and was engaged by *R 195*. Of the 17-man crew aboard the British vessel, six were wounded and one killed. The motor launch diverted to Alinda Bay, disembarked casualties, and then made for the Turkish coast. When barely two miles (3km) from Leros, she was again targeted, this time by the island's shore batteries. Although severely damaged, the ML succeeded in reaching the safety of Turkish waters later that morning.

As well as BYMS 72, the Royal Navy suffered a further loss after three motor launches were ordered to proceed from Leros to Turkish waters. MLs 299 and 461 reached

Not what it might seem. These bombs appear to be falling on Punte Agistro at the southern entrance of Portolago (now Lakki). The target is actually Mericcia on the opposite (northern) side of the bay. (Author's collection)

Leros: Bill Smith, a British LRDG signaller in R1 (New Zealand) patrol, at battery P.L. 113 atop Point 226 (Zuncona). The patrol relocated to LRDG A Squadron HQ after this position was bombed on 9 October. (Brendan O'Carroll)

their destination without mishap but at 0515hrs the latter received a signal from ML 358 that she was being fired on by a convoy. ML 358 was not heard from again. (Five of the crew survived as prisoners of war.)

It was nearly dawn when those on Leros stood to and prepared to face the long-awaited German invasion. On nearing Leros, the eastern force had split into three groups, with Kampfgruppe Dörr making for Palma Bay, Kampfgruppe von Saldern heading towards Grifo Bay and Kampfgruppe Schädlich steering for Appetici. When the latter reached the rocky shore below the imposing heights of Point 180, the Küstenjäger scrambled from their assault boats, out of sight and virtually unopposed by Italian forces on the summit. However, an I-Boot, forced to take up the rear because of engine trouble, came under heavy artillery fire from the battery on Mount Vigla. With no other option, the coxswain manoeuvred the craft inshore. No sooner had the troops disembarked than the vessel was hit and caught fire. This resulted in the Küstenjäger losing their entire stock of spare ammunition. With the burning hulk billowing smoke behind them, and with the grey cliff face towering above, the troops prepared to ascend Appetici and assault Battery Lago.

II./Gren.Rgt. 65 (less two platoons of 5. Kompanie), 131 officers and men of II./Lw.-Jäger-Rgt. 22 and 2./Pi.Btl. 22 (less one platoon) came ashore near Pasta di Sopra Point (6. Kompanie of II./Gren.Rgt. 65 having already suffered losses when an F-lighter took a direct hit). At Grifo Bay, landing craft shot up a battle-damaged British 'gun boat' (this may have been ML 358) and captured the Italian MAS 555 and MAS 559 (both were subsequently lost). At Alinda, the Germans also seized the British LCM 923 (Landing Craft Mechanised).

The remainder of Kampfgruppe von Saldern attempted to force a landing in the Blefuti Bay area, overlooked by Clidi and Battery Ciano. During her approach, Pionierlandungsboot 'H' was damaged by shellfire and drifted close to the islet of Strongilo, just north of Blefuti. Atop Clidi were 15 men of B Squadron LRDG under Capt. John Olivey. Co-located was a Forward Observation Officer of the Royal Artillery who could call on four 25-pdr field guns in the Blacutera area (between San Giovanni and Meraviglia). The 25-pdrs with their high trajectory had been ranged on Strongilo just days before. The Pi-La-Boot had little chance and was soon sunk. Of two officers and 51 ORs of II./Lw.-Jäger-Rgt. 22, at least two ORs were killed and four were wounded. Survivors clambered ashore at Strongilo. One officer and 31 ORs were later taken prisoner. (Four other ranks were accounted for after the fighting was over.)

Another landing craft entered nearby Palma Bay and disembarked two platoons of 5. Kompanie – within Bren gun range of Olivey's force. Men were killed even as the landing craft beached. The situation was critical. Both wireless operators were lost. The company was without communications and a mile from their comrades farther east. Less than a mile to the west was D Company of the Buffs, and above loomed Clidi.

Owing to the encounter with BYMS 72 meanwhile, precious time had been lost before the western force could continue. With coast defences alerted, the flotilla began taking artillery fire while still some 7 miles (11km) from Leros. After three attempts to reach Gurna Bay, with no let-up in the fire from shore, Weissenborn withdrew the force to Kalymnos. Further attempts to reach Leros resulted in casualties and increasing damage to assault craft and escort vessels. The situation was hopeless and eventually Weissenborn was again forced to return to Kalymnos.

Shortly before 0645hrs, Kampfgruppe Dörr had turned back under heavy fire. During a second attempt nearly three hours later, the leading F-lighter received two direct hits, which left at least eight men dead and up to 49 wounded. When the guns switched fire to the accompanying Pi-La-Boot, it, too, was forced to veer away. Unable to press on under such conditions, the force diverted towards Pharmako.

Those landing craft that had managed to disembark their troops faced a hazardous return trip to Kalymnos. Some were unable to break out and instead had to seek shelter close to the coast of Leros where, at least, they were safe from artillery fire.

It had been the intention of Generallt. Müller to land each group simultaneously and to seize control of central Leros before defending forces could recover from their initial surprise. Instead, only part of the invasion force had been put ashore and not necessarily at the designated points. Until he was sure of the situation, Müller would not risk deploying paratroopers. Kampfgruppe Kühne, with approximately 430 men, was en route from mainland Greece when the drop was aborted. No sooner had the Ju 52 transports returned to land, however, than they were ordered to take off again and return to Leros.

At Appetici, the *Küstenjäger* had begun their ascent, remaining unseen by those on the summit until they neared their objective and began to attract small arms fire. The second in command at Battery Lago, S.Ten. Corrado Spagnolo, led the defence until he was mortally wounded later in the day.

View from atop Point 320 (Clidi), a dominating height in northern Leros. The prominent feature on the left is Point 278. Across the bay is Point 189 and Pandeli castle, overlooking the town of Pandeli. The hill behind and left of Point 189 is Point 180. (Appetici)

When the seriousness of the situation became evident, an Italian navy platoon under Ten. 'Ercole' Rocchi rushed to assist from nearby Pandeli castle. The Germans called for air support and by 0930hrs two of the gun emplacements had been taken. Under the battery commander, Cap. Ernesto Nasti, the two remaining guns continued firing.

As the *Küstenjäger* were negotiating the steep slopes of Appetici, Lt. E. B. W. (Ted) Johnson commanding 13 Platoon of the Faughs was called to C Company Headquarters. There, Johnson was told by the company commander, Maj. Ben Barrington, that his platoon was to spearhead a counter-attack and re-take Appetici. By 1000hrs, Johnson's men had reached the summit. Barrington then arrived and ordered Johnson to push on towards Battery Lago, all four guns of which were by then reported to be in German hands. Numbers 1 and 2 guns were taken, thereby securing the narrow plateau atop Appetici (guns 3 and 4 were lower down, on the eastern slope). Johnson and his men reorganized a short distance farther on and there they remained, under continuous Stuka attack, for the rest of the day.

Three miles (5km) north-west of Appetici, there was fighting for several hours as 18 Platoon D Company of the Buffs attempted to repel the half-company of II./Gren.Rgt. 65. The heights overlooking the east side of Palma Bay were initially defended by 8 Section led by Cpl. Bertie C. D. Reed. When the Germans attempted to break out of the confined beachhead, Reed was killed and the section withdrew inland to the area of nearby Point 95. The platoon commander, Lt. Eric J. Ransley, was with the remainder of his men at nearby Blefuti Bay. That morning, an overhead shell-burst had left the officer with a shrapnel wound to his left arm. In spite of the injury, Ransley made ready to confront an enemy twice the strength of his own force. With mortars providing supporting fire, the infantry advanced. When it was over, Ransley's platoon had taken at least 47 prisoners.

The rest of II./Gren.Rgt. 65 and the remainder of II./Lw.-Jäger-Rgt. 22 had pushed inland towards Mount Vedetta. In view of the strategic importance of Clidi, Brig. Tilney had earlier decided to strengthen the position with the Fortress Reserve C Company of the King's Own. On arriving, the company commander, Maj. W. P. T. Tilly, positioned 13 Platoon with two Vickers machine guns atop a ridge in front of an Italian barracks and some 350 yards west of Battery Ciano. Soon afterwards, the area was subjected to mortar and machine-gun fire and low-level aerial dive-bombing. The remaining platoons were deployed in an effort to counter the enemy advance. 14 Platoon was directed left and 15 Platoon right to Point 192. The plan went awry almost from the start, when 14 Platoon withdrew after coming under fire. 15 Platoon was not seen again. At 1045hrs, Fortress Headquarters acknowledged the presence of German troops on Points 217 and 188 on the Vedetta feature, as well as on Point 192. The latter is part of a prominent ridgeline that extends from the coast, north-west to Point 278 and Clidi. Indicating, perhaps, the whereabouts of 15 Platoon and lead elements of Kampfgruppe von Saldern, half an hour later, small arms fire and mortaring was reported around Point 278 and on the southern face of the feature. Fortress Headquarters now ordered that Clidi was to be held at all costs.

On the lower northern slopes of Point 112, south-west of Clidi, Capt. Ashley M. Greenwood, liaison officer between the LRDG and SBS Maj. George Jellicoe, had that morning joined T/Maj Alan Redfern and three LRDG patrols. These were operating in conjunction with SBS, both formations having been tasked by Tilney with providing a mobile force for reconnaissance, patrolling and to deal with paratrooper landings. The total comprised about 28 LRDG officers and ORs, some 30 SBS, and five Greek Sacred Squadron.

Kampfgruppe Kühne had been recalled from mainland Greece as soon as it was known that German forces had gained a foothold on Leros. At about 1430hrs, an impressive air armada began its approach from the west at wave-top height: some three dozen transports in line ahead escorted by

Arado floatplanes, Ju 87s and Ju 88s. A number of low-flying aircraft appeared over central Leros to strafe and scatter anti-personnel bombs. The slower transports followed. As parachutes descended south of their position, those atop Clidi opened fire with everything they had. The landing was also opposed by D Company of the Faughs from Point 36, Germano and San Giovanni; by B Company of the Royal West Kents at San Giovanni, and by the Buffs at lower Quirico. The paratroopers – about 430 – sustained losses of around ten per cent during and immediately after their descent.

The drop zone chosen for German paratroopers was in low ground between the bays of Alinda and Gurna, seen here from the road to Clidi. The hill lower right is Point 184/Quirico. (Author's collection)

One of the Ju 52s crashed just inland of Alinda Bay: only the wireless operator escaped with his life. (During air operations between 12 and 16 November, the Luftwaffe would lose at least 12 aircraft.)

15 Platoon of the King's Own had the misfortune to encounter some of Kühne's *Fallschirmjäger* south of Clidi, on the northernmost fringe of the drop zone. Among those killed was the platoon commander, Lt. Desmond P. R. Ginn.

A short distance away, at Point 112, SBS had positioned three M.G. 15s overlooking the likely drop zone. They were soon in action, together with machine guns manned by LRDG. Within minutes the SBS patrol took its first casualty when a Greek officer was wounded by return fire. A hasty redeployment went badly, resulting in casualties, including the death of Alan Redfern.

After gathering all available *Fallschirmjäger*, Kühne swiftly secured his primary objectives. Supported by Stukas, 1. Kompanie covered the northern area, severing all roads and lines of communication; 2. and 4. Kompanie took Rachi at the first attempt; to the west of Alinda Bay 3. Kompanie cut off the road between Platanos and Partheni, and reconnoitred northward. Within the drop zone, only 17 Platoon of the Faughs continued to hold out at Germano.

At Olivey's position, the situation was quickly deteriorating. On nearby Vedetta, 7./Lw.-Jäger-Rgt. 22, together with part of 6. Kompanie, had received orders to join an attack on Clidi, moving south-west over the ridge between Points 234 and 264, and across to Point 228. By 1500hrs, they were in an open valley below their objective. Just over an hour later, German infantry reached Point 278, just south-east of Battery Ciano. As the enemy closed in, the LRDG withdrew, but not before setting a delayed charge that would destroy one of the battery guns.

By late evening, Kampfgruppe von Saldern had achieved its objectives, holding the high ground stretching from Point 234 (Vedetta) through Points 228 and 320 (Clidi) to 550 yards west of Santa Madonna (Alinda Bay). With Kühne's paratroopers in control of most of the key points south of Clidi, the Germans had effectively divided the island in two.

There were two parachute drops. The first was on 12 November and involved a mass drop. The second was a day later, when each Ju 52 arrived singly. Both operations were carried out under heavy fire. (Author's collection)

Earlier, Tilney had moved three companies of the King's Own from the southern coastal region to high ground in support of the gun positions on Scumbarda, and to the east of Serocampo Bay, leaving medium machine guns to assist the Italians on the beaches. Towards the end of the day, when it became apparent that the enemy's main effort was being concentrated in the centre of the island between Clidi and Appetici, the King's Own was again redeployed, three companies going to the Meraviglia area, and one company moving from the north shore of Lakki to positions covering Point 248 (Patella). Considering the Germans at Appetici to have been contained, Tilney also recalled C Company of the Faughs from their hard-won positions at Battery Lago. The withdrawal of C Company prompted an appeal by the Italian command, fearing that without British help the feature could not be held. 15 Platoon (C Company) was directed to return to Appetici, presumably by Tilney. The order seems to have been passed directly to the platoon, thus bypassing the normal chain of command and leaving the battalion and company commanders in ignorance.

At the time, Lt. Col. French is thought to have been with Maj. Barrington preparing for a night operation to push the enemy off Rachi. There are conflicting and confusing accounts about why the attack did not materialize. The most likely scenario is that 13 and 14 Platoons of the Faughs were allocated two simultaneous tasks: to attack Rachi and to return to Appetici in support of 15 Platoon. If this is indeed what occurred, then in the British camp, after just one day of battle, command and control were already breaking down.

# 13 NOVEMBER

On Friday night (the 12th), Cdr. Stuart A. Buss, RN, 5th Destroyer Flotilla, arrived in the Aegean in HMS *Dulverton*, with *Echo* and *Belvoir* in attendance. After being detected and shadowed by German aircraft, the unit was attacked with glide bombs and at about 0145hrs on the 13th *Dulverton* was hit and her bows blown away. Subsequently, she was torpedoed and sunk by HMS *Belvoir*.

On the 13th, strong winds would result in the Luftwaffe scaling down activities over Leros and also prevent small craft from operating. Early in the morning, and before the weather had worsened, Kampfgruppe Aschoff with II./Gren.Rgt. 16 attempted another landing, this time on the northern coast. Initially, the attention of shore defences was diverted when the patrolling MTBs 315 and 266 were mistakenly illuminated and fired on. It was the second occasion that night that the torpedo boats had been wrongly targeted. They withdrew from the area and therefore failed to intercept the German

## Leros, 13 November 1943

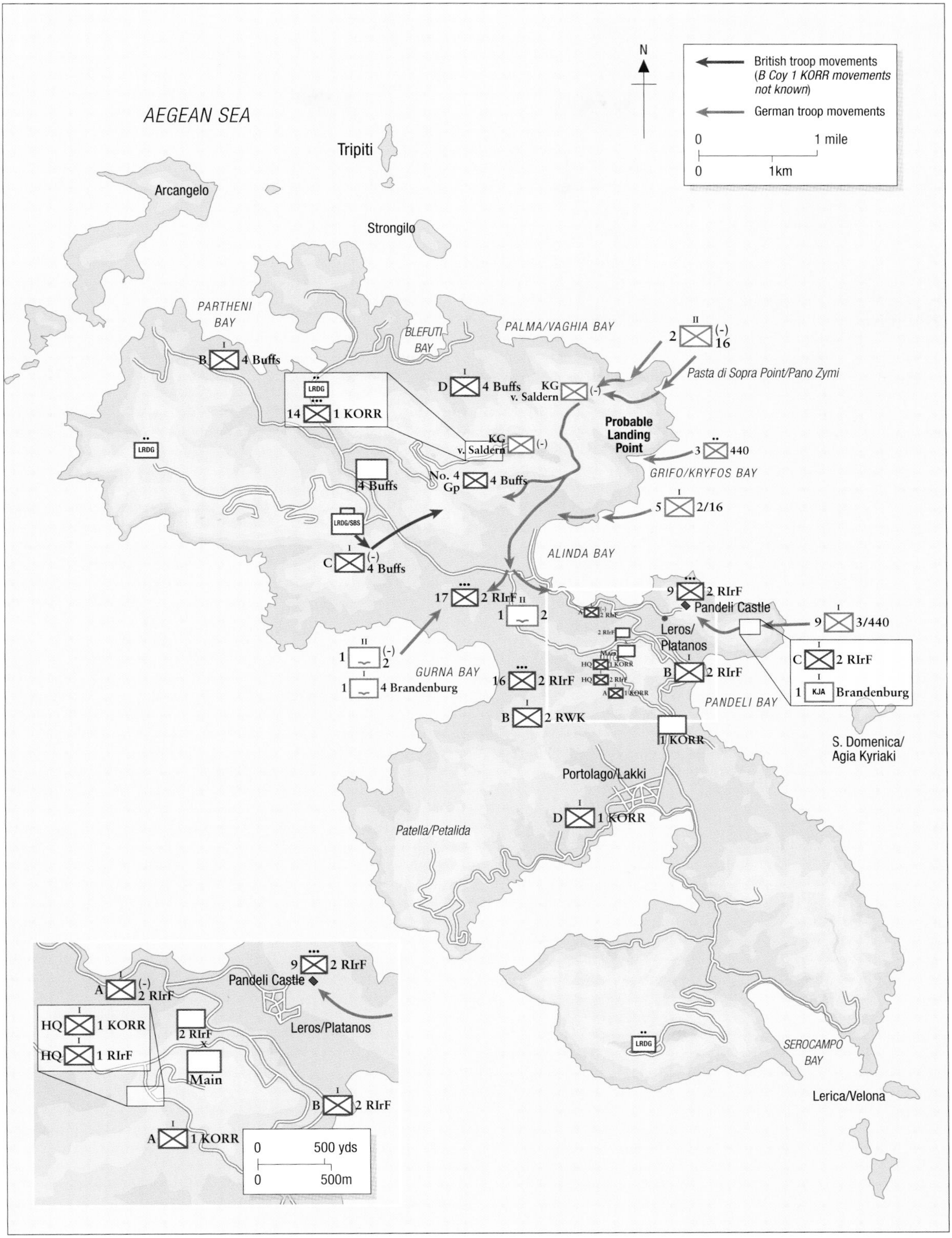

British troop movements (B Coy 1 KORR movements not known)
German troop movements
0 1 mile
0 1km
N
AEGEAN SEA
Tripiti
Arcangelo
Strongilo
PARTHENI BAY
BLEFUTI BAY
PALMA/VAGHIA BAY
Pasta di Sopra Point/Pano Zymi
Probable Landing Point
GRIFO/KRYFOS BAY
ALINDA BAY
GURNA BAY
PANDELI BAY
Pandeli Castle
Leros/Platanos
S. Domenica/Agia Kyriaki
Portolago/Lakki
Patella/Petalida
SEROCAMPO BAY
Lerica/Velona
B 4 Buffs
D 4 Buffs
LRDG
14 1 KORR
KG v. Saldern (-)
2 (-) 16
3 440
No. 4 Gp 4 Buffs
4 Buffs
5 2/16
LRDG/SBS
C (-) 4 Buffs
17 2 RIrF
1 2
1 (-) 2
1 4 Brandenburg
16 2 RIrF
B 2 RWK
9 2 RIrF
9 3/440
C 2 RIrF
1 KJA Brandenburg
B 2 RIrF
1 KORR
D 1 KORR
A (-) 2 RIrF
HQ 1 KORR
HQ 1 RIrF
2 RIrF
Main
A 1 KORR
0 500 yds
0 500m

Known to the British as 'the Anchor', this was and still is the main junction connecting Lakki in the centre of Leros with Platanos, Meraviglia, Alinda and the route north-west to Partheni. (Author's collection)

flotilla. A landing was made near Pasta di Sopra Point at daybreak. One landing craft was disabled and drifted with a damaged rudder close to Santa Madonne in Alinda Bay, where she was hit by Bofors and anti-tank guns from the southern shore and set on fire. The flames spread, detonating onboard ammunition. Those who were able escaped overboard and struggled to reach the coast 200 yards away. The remnants of the battalion gathered on the eastern slope of Vedetta until ordered by Maj. von Saldern to advance via Val Camere (south of Clidi) towards Rachi to link up with the *Fallschirmjäger*.

Following the failure of Kampfgruppe Dörr to reach Palma Bay the previous day, III./Gren.Rgt. 440 also benefited from the diversion resulting from the British MTBs, before coming under heavy artillery fire while trying to land at Appetici. Only 9. Kompanie succeeded in getting ashore and at 0630hrs joined up with the *Küstenjäger* on the eastern slope. About 30 men of 10. and 11. Kompanie also landed north of Grifo Bay, where they were incorporated into II./Gren.Rgt. 16. Having lost one engine, and prevented by rough seas from reaching shore, the remaining landing craft returned to Kalymnos, shipping water and with the occupants bailing with their steel helmets in order to stay afloat.

Unfavourable weather conditions delayed a proposed pre-dawn parachute assault until 0645hrs, when 15./4.Rgt. 'Brandenburg' and about 40 men of I./Fallschirmjäger-Rgt. 2 were dropped west of Rachi. The paratroopers suffered heavy losses. One stick was dropped at such a low altitude that none of the parachutes opened in time. Another stick fell into the sea. Ground fire accounted for at least two Ju 52s.

At Appetici, a concerted effort by the *Küstenjäger* and 9./Gren.Rgt. 440 saw all four guns of the battery and a number of British and Italians overrun at 1100hrs. Lieutenant Ted Johnson, on the north-west slope of the summit, was informed of the situation and soon afterwards experienced substantial rifle and machine-gun fire. The Faughs withdrew in disorder, leaving Appetici to the enemy. The loss of Appetici caused considerable difficulties for B Company of the Faughs, whose area at Pandeli, south of the feature, was now overlooked and dominated by German forces.

At about midday, two companies of Gren.Rgt. 16 descended the southern slopes of Point 192. Part of 6. Kompanie cleared the southern face of Point 111 (between Clidi and Quirico), before continuing south with 7. Kompanie towards Rachi. Pockets of resistance encountered along the way were dealt with during close-quarter fighting. Shortly before 1600hrs, III. Zug of 7. Kompanie met up with *Fallschirmjäger* at San Nicola, and the latter was placed under the command of II./Gren.Rgt. 16. The southern shore of Alinda was a scene of further actions during the afternoon.

There was also activity in the vicinity of Point 320 when, at dawn, German forces prevented an attempted breakthrough just south of the height. Between 0730 and 0800hrs a second attack was beaten back with grenades and small arms fire. Those responsible may have been from HQ Company (or No. 4 Group) of the Buffs, who were tasked with securing Point 184 (Quirico). Certainly, Quirico fell to German forces at some point during the day, prompting an unsuccessful attempt by part of C Company of the Buffs to recapture the feature that night.

Earlier, the SBS and Y, T1 and T2 Patrols of the LRDG had been placed under the command of Lt. Col. Douglas Iggulden, and were redeployed just north of the Buffs C Company positions on Mount Condrida. During the 13th (and for much of the battle) most of the LRDG and SBS seem to have avoided being saddled with infantry tasks, other than to take over night-time infantry positions.

At the end of day two of the battle, German forces held Appetici and had established a pocket around Alinda, from the coast at Vedetta, south-west past Clidi to Quirico and south-east to Germano, Rachi and towards Krithoni. However, an attempt during the afternoon to take Pandeli castle had failed in the face of Allied artillery, mortar and machine-gun fire. Neither had Kampfgruppe von Saldern linked up with the *Küstenjäger* and 9./Gren. Rgt. 440 at Appetici, which was crucial if Alinda Bay was to be secured for the landing of heavy weapons.

In the north, Clidi battery was in German hands. Iggulden was instructed by Brig. Tilney to retake the height that night, and to be prepared to move south the following day and secure the northern slopes of Rachi. In fact, Iggulden had made up his own mind to restore the situation at Clidi, and since communication problems prevented him from maintaining contact with the brigadier, intended to proceed at dawn on the 14th. In the meantime B and C Companies of the Buffs were withdrawn from their positions, the former to seize Clidi, and the latter to counterattack at Quirico. Captain Denniff and Y Patrol took over from B Company at Partheni that evening, and during the night the remainder of the LRDG and SBS replaced C Company on the Condrida feature. D Company of the Buffs was ordered to move south to the central area.

At Germano, 17 Platoon of the Faughs remained in position until about 2000hrs, when, under orders from Battalion Heaquarters, Sgt. Daniel P. O'Connell withdrew the men through B Company of the Royal West Kents. The enemy chose this moment to attack, causing the platoon to leave without its wounded.

Meanwhile, the Faughs' 16 Platoon had been placed under command of Capt. E. P. (Percy) Flood OC B Company. During the day the platoon commander, Lt. Prior, was wounded. He was

This image by Propagandakompanie photographer Schilling appeared in the Wehrmacht newssheet *Wacht im Südosten*. According to the original caption these men are taking cover during an attack by their own Ju 87s. The location is almost certainly battery P.L. 211 on Rachi. (Author's collection)

replaced by Lt. S. A. (Arthur) Stokes, a South African on secondment to the British Army and attached to HQ Company of the Faughs. During the afternoon Stokes had led an attack in which an estimated 20 Germans were killed and wounded.

For Tilney the loss of Appetici represented as serious a threat to Meraviglia as did the German occupation of Rachi. In the morning, he had therefore issued instructions for Lt. Col. French and Lt. Col. S. A. F. S. Egerton, commanding the King's Own, to prepare for a night attack on Appetici. As he was familiar with the terrain, the CO of the Faughs was asked to co-ordinate the plan. He then surprised all involved by announcing that he would lead the attack in place of Egerton. Slightly below and west of Battery Lago are several windmills. This was to be the start line. It was intended to clear Appetici shortly after moonrise. The King's Own provided all three companies, each with a guide from the Faughs. Lieutenant Robert (Austin) Ardill, who had previously commanded the Faughs' Anti-Tank Platoon on Appetici, was to take charge of the lead A Company and secure searchlight and gun positions. D Company was to follow up on the left and clear the tunnel system beneath the battery. HQ Company would form a semi-circle behind the attacking companies and prevent enemy forces from escaping. Before dawn, A and D Companies were to withdraw to 'the Anchor' in order to be available for further offensive operations towards Rachi, leaving HQ Company to organize and hold the position. (The Anchor, or Porta Vecchia, was the main road junction linking Lakki with central and northern Leros.)

# 14 NOVEMBER

Late on the 13th, Lt. Col. French led the King's Own up the steep southern face of Appetici. As he neared the top, French was recalled in order to come to the aid of Fortress Headquarters, said to be under threat from a German attack. Deciding it was too risky to turn back the entire force without being detected, French instead instructed HQ Company at the rear to return. The panic was probably due to a company of I./Fallschirmjäger-Rgt. 2, reinforced by troops of II./Gren.Rgt. 16, having been tasked with taking Point 101, on the western edge of the Meraviglia feature. But, as a result, the Appetici assault force was significantly reduced.

Soon after midnight, the British destroyers *Echo* and *Belvoir* arrived off Alinda Bay and commenced a ten-minute preliminary bombardment of Appetici. For whatever reason, the ground attack did not begin until later, at approximately 0230hrs. Conditions were hardly ideal. They benefited and, to a degree, hindered the attackers. Because of the featureless terrain it can be difficult even in daylight to determine exactly where one is on Appetici's slopes. In common with much of the island, the landscape is extremely rugged, rocky and covered with Greek spiny spurge, a dense, thorny, low-lying plant. Negotiating this natural obstacle can be a slow, frustrating and painful experience. Appetici is miserable when the weather deteriorates. In high winds, the exposed slopes offer no shelter and one soon becomes disorientated. Maurice French and his force had this to contend with and more: the men were unfamiliar with the area, tired after two days of activity and hardly enthusiastic about attacking a resolute enemy.

# Leros, 14 November 1943

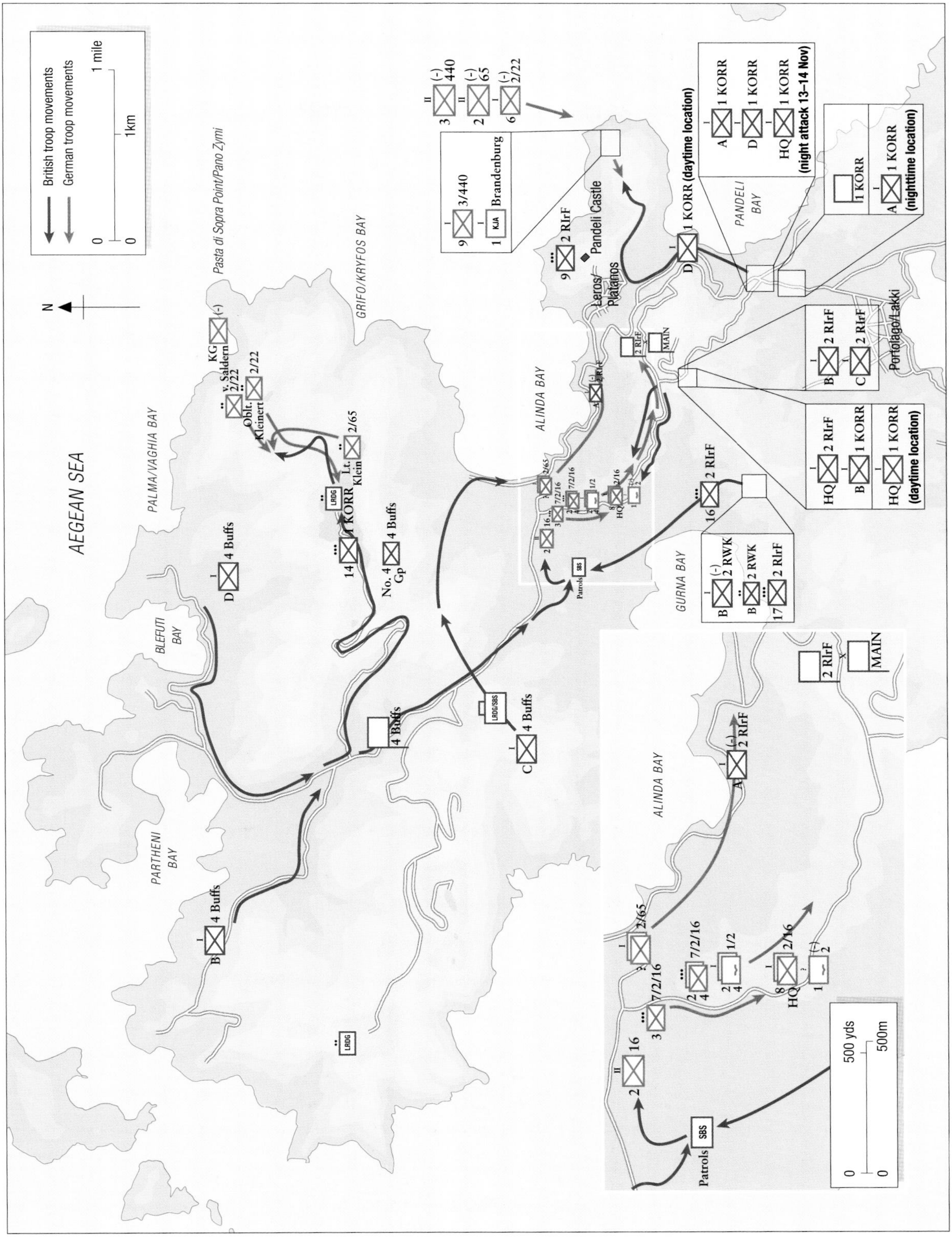

British troop movements
German troop movements
0
1 mile
0
1km
N
AEGEAN SEA
PALMA/VAGHIA BAY
BLEFUTI BAY
PARTHENI BAY
GRIFO/KRYFOS BAY
ALINDA BAY
GURNA BAY
PANDELI BAY
Pasta di Sopra Point/Pano Zymi
KG v. Saldern (-)
2/22
2/22
Oblt. Kleinert
2/65
Lt. Klein
LRDG
14 1 KORR
No. 4 Gp 4 Buffs
D 4 Buffs
B 4 Buffs
4 Buffs
C 4 Buffs
LRDG/SBS
LRDG
Patrols SBS
16 2 RIrF
B 2 RWK (-)
B 2 RWK
17 2 RIrF
HQ 2 RIrF
B 1 KORR
HQ 1 KORR (daytime location)
B 2 RIrF
C 2 RIrF
Portolago/Lakki
2 RIrF
MAIN
Leros/Platanos
9 2 RIrF
Pandeli Castle
D 1 KORR
1 KORR (daytime location)
9 3/440
1 KJA Brandenburg
3 440 (-)
2 65 (-)
6 2/22 (-)
A 1 KORR
D 1 KORR
HQ 1 KORR
(night attack 13–14 Nov)
1 KORR
A 1 KORR
(nighttime location)
A 2 RIrF (-)
2/65
7/2/16
3 7/2/16
2 4
1/2
8 HQ 2/16
1 2 (-)
2 16
Patrols
SBS
0
500 yds
0
500m

The close proximity of Allied and Axis forces during the battle for Leros meant that no one was safe in the open, as is apparent in this evocative image of a German paratrooper. (Author's collection)

Although two of its platoons had disappeared during the night, having no doubt lost their way in the dark, A Company managed to get as far as the first gun position before German machine-gunners found their range. Progress was slow. D Company also got into difficulties, having to resort to platoon attacks under machine-gun and mortar fire. On top of the feature, close fighting served only to confuse the situation. Just before dawn, the Kommandeur of 9./Gren.Rgt. 440 led a counter-attack, pushing back the King's Own.

Fifty-five British and 45 Italians (presumably battery personnel) were taken prisoner. Among those killed was the much-respected CO of the Faughs, Lt. Col. French. D Company was withdrawn a short distance to Vromolito, where it took over from the Royal Irish Fusiliers. Some survivors of A Company apparently retreated as far south as Scumbarda, before being ordered to return to the Anchor area.

At 0600hrs, Kampfgruppe von Saldern prepared to push from Rachi towards Meraviglia with 2. and 4. Kompanie of Kühne's *Fallschirmjäger*. Troops of II./Gren.Rgt. 65 were deployed along the coast road of Alinda Bay, while II./Gren.Rgt. 16 was tasked with securing a line from Point 22, on the road between Quirico and Germano, through Germano and Rachi. II./Lw.-Jäger-Rgt. 22 with elements of III./Gren.Rgt. 440 and 6./Gren.Rgt. 65 was to establish a line from Mount Vedetta through Clidi, Quirico and the area south. During their assault, the paratroopers were covered by a captured Italian anti-aircraft gun (almost certainly P.L. 211 on Rachi), and by 0700hrs had reached Points 108 and 113 north and west of Meraviglia's summit. Two companies of II./Gren.Rgt. 65 also advanced east and established a line from Santa Marina on the coast, to Point 108. But further moves by the Germans were thwarted when they were forced to call off their offensive and re-deploy in response to a simultaneous effort by British troops to recover lost ground with the intention of destroying German forces in the Rachi area and containing those on Appetici.

Lieutenant-Colonel Iggulden's morning attack against Hptm. Gawlich's force on Clidi was a success. Led by Maj. Ernest A. Hole, and supported by artillery and mortars, B Company of the Buffs advanced east from Point 252 and by 0725hrs had taken the height and with it some 40 prisoners.

For their part, Capt. Olivey's LRDG were tasked initially with clearing a cave on the east side of Point 320, taking 15 or so prisoners in the process. The LRDG was then divided into three-man teams to guide the Buffs in an area sweep. The British took a number of casualties, including 2/Lt. Thomas L. Morgan, who was killed.

It had originally been intended for B Company of the Buffs to push on to the north shore of Alinda and there link up with the battalion's C Company, after the latter had arrived by way of Quirico. Instead, B Company would spend the day trying to dislodge the enemy from high ground, for, as soon as Clidi was overrun, II./Lw.-Jäger-Rgt. 22 was ordered to re-take the height.

At 1100hrs, Oblt. Kleinert with an assault group of 18 men (mainly wireless operators, clerks and kitchen personnel) launched an attack from Mount Vedetta, south past Point 228 and towards the razor-edged 278. While passing a trench south-east of 228, one man was badly wounded by sniper fire from the dominating massif of Point 320. The rest of the force went to ground. Before long, Lt. Klein of II./Gren.Rgt. 65 arrived with another group and agreed to attempt to reach Clidi from the south. No sooner had Klein's men moved out, however, than they were engaged from the southern slopes of 228. Kleinert's group returned fire. This, in turn, attracted the attention of a machine-gunner, who accounted for several killed and wounded. Those who could do so withdrew from the exposed valley, south towards Point 278.

After reorganizing his men, Klein, together with a ten-man reserve under the commanding officer of II./Lw.-Jäger-Rgt. 22, proceeded to clear Point 228. They pushed the defenders into a nearby ravine but, after coming under mortar and machine-gun fire from Point 320, had to seek cover in dead ground behind the height. The Germans had failed to recapture Point 320, but neither did the Buffs manage to advance past Point 192. Several Germans had been wounded, three of them seriously, including Klein. Among the British dead was Ernest Hole. Lieutenant Bill Taylor took over as company commander for the remainder of the day. Eventually the Buffs fell back on Olivey's position, which was to remain in Allied hands for the duration of the battle.

By midday, C Company of the Buffs under Maj. V. G. 'Pistol' Bourne had taken Quirico and a number of prisoners (accounts vary from more than 30 to more than 60). The company proceeded east to Alinda Bay before changing direction towards Villa Belleni and, after skirmishing through the gardens and houses on the west side of Alinda, penetrated the line held by I. Zug of 7./Gren.Rgt. 16. Prevented by communication problems from requesting close artillery support, the Buffs were unable to exploit the situation, and in the face of determined resistance the advance inevitably faltered.

In the morning, Brig. Tilney had briefed the commanding officers of the King's Own and the Faughs (the latter now under Maj. Bill Shephard) for an attack on Rachi. B and C Companies of the Faughs, assisted by B and HQ Companies of the King's Own, were to clear the ridge north-west to Point 100, while B Company of the Royal West Kents, with 16 Platoon of the Faughs attached, advanced west past the feature to Germano. Once Rachi was clear, the Fortress Commander proposed personally to co-ordinate its organization. The attack commenced at about 0930hrs, with C Company as spearhead making good headway and taking a number of prisoners, while the Faughs' B Company advanced along the opposite side of the ridge. The two King's Own companies were apparently delayed by

*Kampfgruppe* commander Hauptmann Martin Kühne, issuing instructions to his men, probably near the end or just after the battle. (Author's collection)

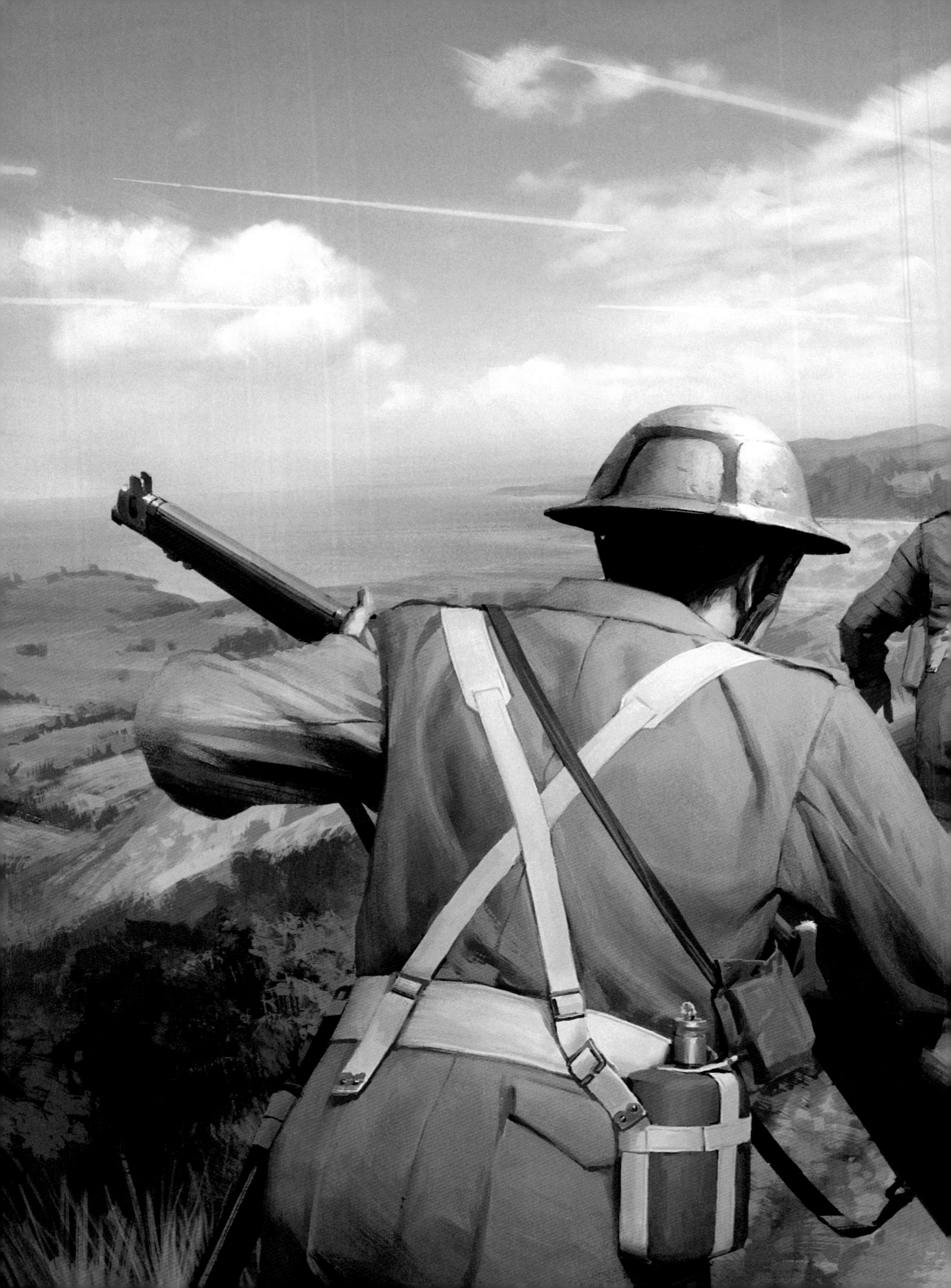

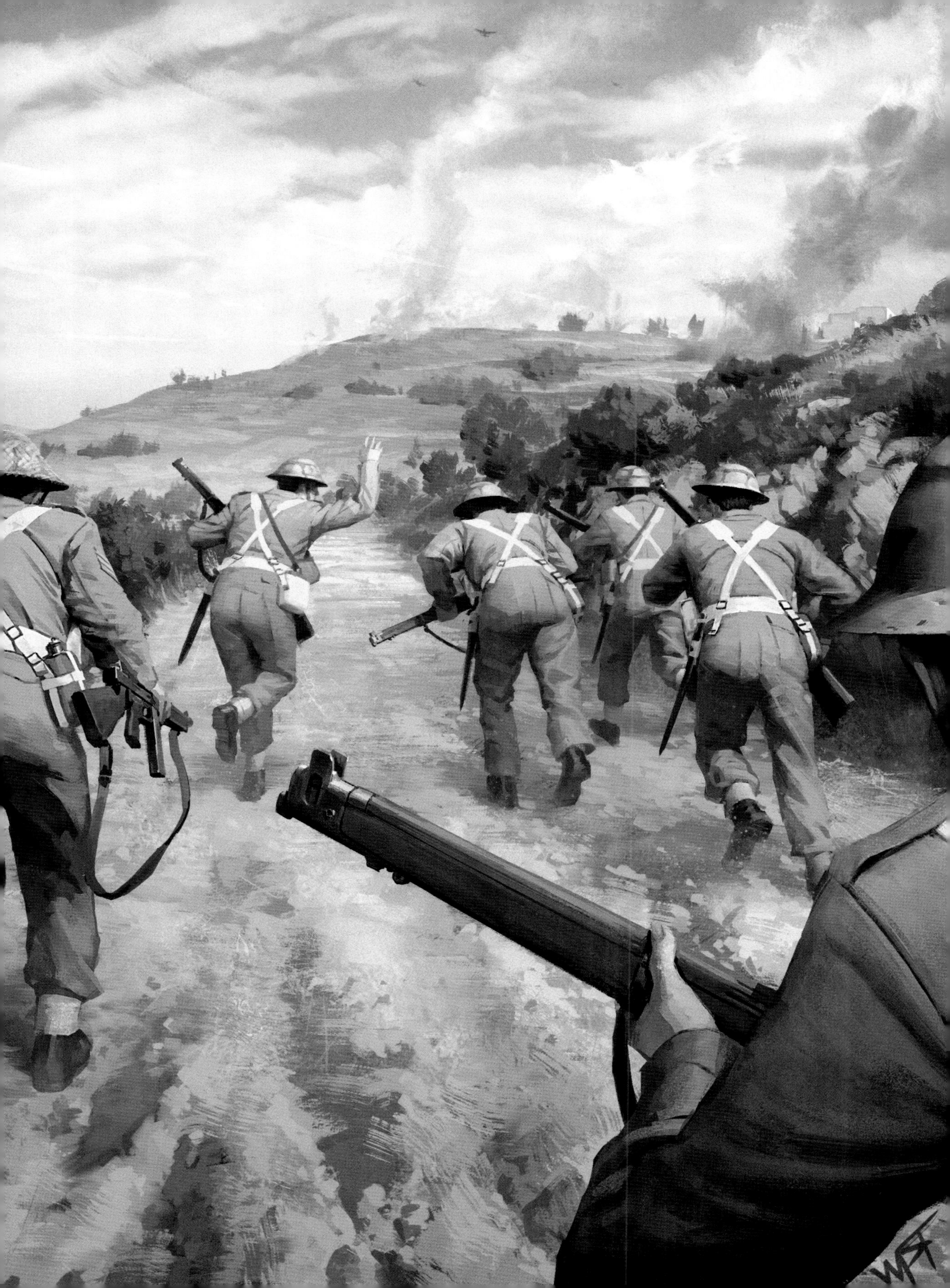

**LIEUTENANT TED JOHNSON'S ASSAULT ALONG RACHI RIDGE, MORNING OF 14 NOVEMBER 1943 (PP. 68–69)**

On 14 November 1943, an attempt was made to clear Rachi Ridge **(1)** of enemy forces. B and C Companies of the Royal Irish Fusiliers were to advance from 'Charing Cross' road junction and clear Rachi's eastern and western slopes respectively. B and HQ Companies of the King's Own were to assist, not least by first securing Point 97, or Searchlight Hill, a small knoll at the eastern end of Rachi Ridge. B Company of the Royal West Kents, together with 16 Platoon of the Faughs, would in the meantime move west, below Rachi, to link up with the Buffs at Germano. The assault began at about 0930hrs. Searchlight Hill was secured and on either side of Rachi, B and C Companies of the Faughs made good headway. The assault was well supported by machine-gun, Bofors and mortar fire. Lt. Ted Johnson's **(2)** and 13 Platoon spearheaded the way for C Company. Johnson had learned that an officer's service revolver was of little use in such a situation and he had by now acquired a rifle. With rifles at the high port, Johnson's platoon advanced along Rachi's western slopes. The platoon commander arrived at his objective in good time, but with little more than half a dozen men, everybody else having tailed behind. The Royal West Kents with the Faughs' 16 Platoon continued towards Germano, which was reached with relatively little trouble. However, on Rachi things were not proceeding as planned. As a result of the British attack, a platoon of 7./Gren.Rgt. 16 was ordered to secure the western end of Rachi. Johnson was soon joined by others of C Company, but any further progress was halted by German forces on Point 100, just above their position. Enemy resistance also put a stop to B Company's advance. Point 109 **(3)**, close by, could not be taken either, due to a counter-attack by German paratroopers and infantry of II./Gren.Rgt. 16. Ju 87 Stukas **(4)** were another threat, orbiting the battlefield so as to be on call to their comrades on the ground. That afternoon, the Faughs pulled back. Costly efforts by the King's Own were also unsuccessful. Rachi Ridge was fought over again the next day, 15 November. But with the exception of Searchlight Hill, German forces managed to control the feature and would continue to do so until being withdrawn and redeployed for the last phase of the battle.

enemy pockets overlooked by C Company. Fighting continued until evening, and ended with Point 97 (Searchlight Hill) in British hands. An effort to take Point 109, just 250 yards away, failed when it met with a counter-attack by German paratroopers, together with 8. Kompanie and Headquarters personnel of II./Gren.Rgt. 16.

To counter the Allied threat, Hptm. Philipp Aschoff ordered III. Zug of 7./Gren.Rgt. 16 to secure the western side of Rachi. By late afternoon both B and C Companies of the Faughs had returned to their original positions. In B Company, at least three had been killed and several more were wounded, including the OC, Capt. C. R. Mason, who was temporarily replaced by Lt. T. West and Maj. Ben Barrington, with command of C Company passing to Lt. Ted Johnson.

Earlier in the day, two SBS patrols had been sent to Germano in order to protect the right (east) flank. It would seem that enemy forces also occupied part of the feature for, at dawn, D Company of the Buffs under Maj. E. W. Tassell had advanced southward only to encounter strong resistance in the area. D Company attacked and took the position shortly before midday. Soon after, D Company was able to marry up with B Company of the Royal West Kents, the latter also coming under Iggulden's command. Subsequently, both companies were directed to nearby San Nicola, with D Company on the right, and B Company left. Wireless problems meant there was no close artillery support during the attack against an enemy which had made a strongpoint of every house in the area. The British infantry were prevented even from penetrating the village outskirts.

With an improvement in the weather, German air support had intensified dramatically on the 14th, with Stukas always on call. Dusk brought with it a respite from air attacks, and a lessening of the shelling that prevailed during daylight hours. But intermittent gunfire continued throughout the night.

After dark, a strong patrol of HQ Company of the Buffs moved into position on Point 111, extending the British line, which stretched west to Clidi and south through Quirico to Germano. The ground from Meraviglia west to Searchlight Hill was also in Allied hands, and so far the Germans were contained on Appetici. To avoid being cut off by a significant British presence on Point 101, Maj. von Saldern pulled back his troops from the north-west slopes of Meraviglia and the line extending from Point 108 to Santa Marina, to a line from Rachi, north to the coast near Patriarcato. A company was also deployed just north of San Quaranta on the west shore of Alinda Bay. Kampfgruppe Müller had suffered substantial losses and had failed to secure a number of key features. Furthermore, there were insufficient German forces to maintain contact between those in the Vedetta–Grifo Bay area and those to the west of Alinda

The eyes say it all. Filthy and unshaven infantrymen of III./Gren.Rgt. 440 show the strain of having come through the fighting on Appetici. (Dr. med. Georg Repp via Verena Repp-Gröpl)

Bay. This left a dangerous breach, which had to be covered throughout the night by reconnaissance patrols. If ever there was a time Tilney might have reversed the situation on Leros, this was it. Unfortunately, he was unaware of the German plight and, with his own forces having also suffered during the day's fighting, did not follow up on their successes.

Müller knew that his *Kampfgruppe* could not hope to continue without heavy weapons, but landing conditions were impossible. The best that could be achieved was to provide ammunition re-supply through continuous airdrops. Late on Sunday afternoon, he issued a revised battle plan: the beachhead at Mount Vedetta–Grifo Bay was to be held until ordered; that at Alinda Bay was to be held until 1400hrs on the 15th. The Luftwaffe would then support a major push via Meraviglia to Pandeli Bay, with the intention of establishing a new beachhead from Pandeli castle through Meraviglia, south to Points 132 and 79, and east to Point 102 (Mount Vigla). Sufficient forces were to remain on Rachi to prevent Allied movement between Alinda and Gurna bays. Furthermore, Hptm. Dörr with troops remaining of III./Gren.Rgt. 440, II./Gren.Rgt. 65 and 6./Lw.-Jäger-Rgt. 22 was to land east of Appetici in the evening of the 14th and take command of the units already there, preparatory to seizing Pandeli castle and linking up with Kampfgruppe von Saldern.

At approximately 1730hrs, the destroyers *Penn*, *Aldenham* and *Blencathra* arrived at Alinda Bay. Soon after, they responded to a request from the island to engage German defensive positions. From onshore, a captured gun was turned against *Penn*. The response was an immediate burst of 20mm cannon fire. The bombardment continued for about 15 minutes, during which both enemy and friendly forces had to take cover. The hospital at Villa Belleni was hit, resulting in the deaths of several patients. In the area of San Quaranta, there were casualties among C Company of the Buffs. The disruption was such that Maj. Bourne considered it impractical to press on and instead pulled back to Point 81, south-east of Quirico.

That night, Dörr and his command were ferried from Kalymnos and deployed below Appetici. British reinforcements were also on the way from Samos. MMS 103 with A Company of the Royal West Kents reached Lakki at 2240hrs. The troops disembarked and moved to a nearby assembly area, while the company commander, Maj. Robert Butler, reported to Fortress Headquarters for orders. The minesweeper remained long enough to take on board wounded before she again put to sea. In the early hours of the 15th, HMS *Echo* disembarked C Company and additional personnel of the Royal West Kents. *Echo* withdrew from Leros as a German effort was under way to evacuate by sea wounded and British prisoners. Also in the area were MTBs 315 and 266. All three vessels engaged the German convoy, sinking MFP 331 and Pi-La-Boot 482/M.

# 15 NOVEMBER

Brigadier Tilney's intentions for the 15th were to annihilate enemy forces in the Rachi–San Quaranta area, and thereafter concentrate the defence in the area of Meraviglia. The final plan would not be decided until later in the day, but essentially called for a two-phase attack involving newly-arrived A and C Companies of the Royal West Kents. Firstly, A Company was to

# Leros, 15 November 1943

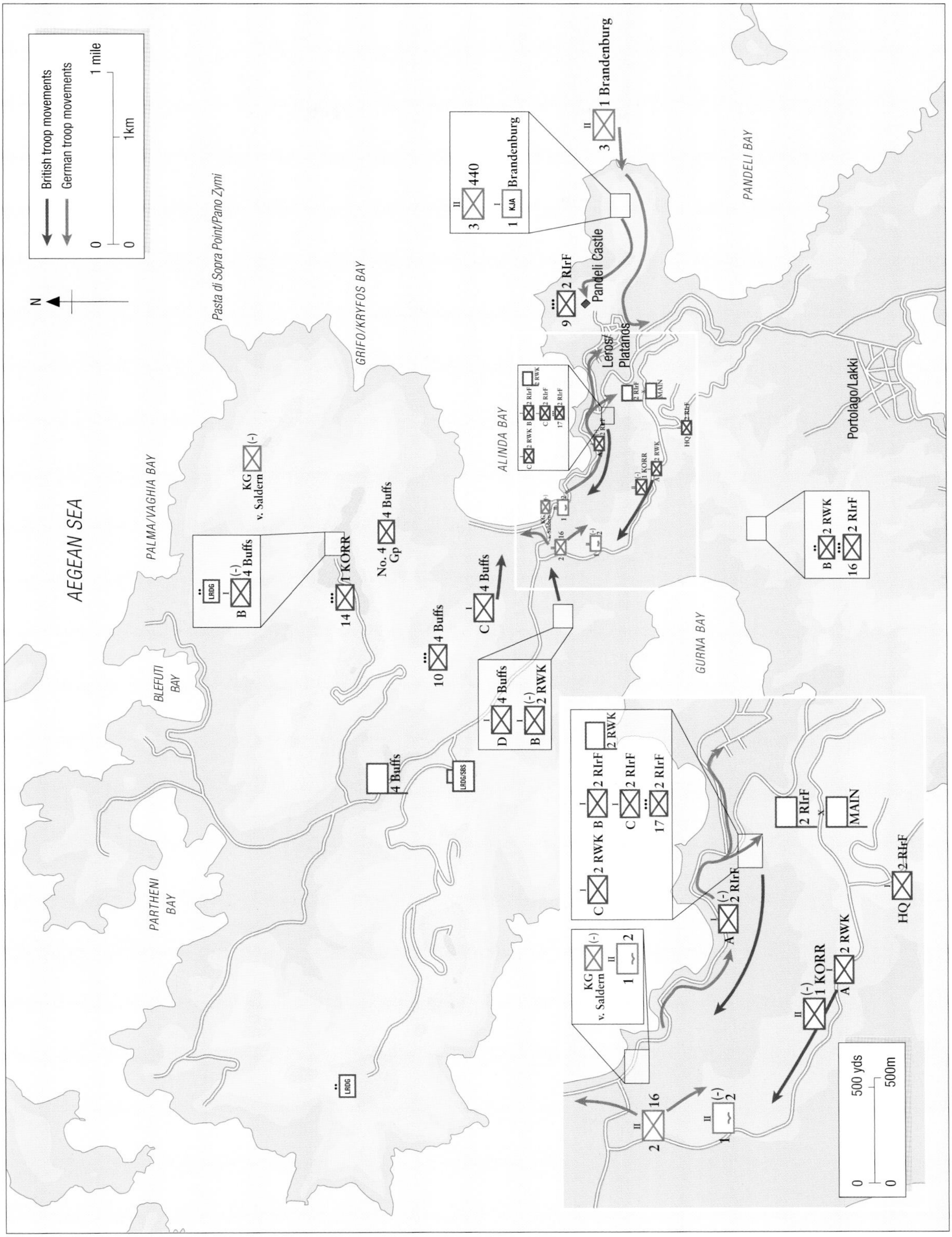
British troop movements
German troop movements
0
1 mile
0
1km
N
AEGEAN SEA
PALMA/VAGHIA BAY
Pasta di Sopra Point/Pano Zymi
GRIFO/KRYFOS BAY
ALINDA BAY
PANDELI BAY
GURNA BAY
BLEFUTI BAY
PARTHENI BAY
Pandeli Castle
Leros/ Platanos
Portolago/Lakki
3 1 Brandenburg
3 440
1 KJA Brandenburg
9 2 RIrF
KG v. Saldern (-)
14 1 KORR
B 4 Buffs (-)
LRDG
No. 4 Gp 4 Buffs
10 4 Buffs
C 4 Buffs
D 4 Buffs
B 2 RWK (-)
4 Buffs
LRDG/SBS
B 2 RWK
16 2 RIrF
C 2 RWK
B 2 RIrF
C 2 RIrF
17 2 RIrF
2 RWK
2 RIrF
MAIN
HQ 2 RIrF
A 2 RIrF (-)
A 2 RWK
1 KORR (-)
KG v. Saldern (-)
1 2
2 16
1 2 (-)
500 yds
500m

pass through the King's Own on Searchlight Hill, with the unenviable task of securing Rachi Ridge from the centre, to the northern limits of Point 100. The King's Own was to follow up and occupy the ridge from the centre, back to Searchlight Hill. On successful completion of the first phase, D Company of the Buffs with B Company of the Royal West Kents were to advance southward to San Quaranta and San Nicola, and drive the enemy towards C Company of the Royal West Kents. The latter was to proceed north-west on a one-company front, with its right flank on the coast road and its left on the eastern slopes of Rachi, and secure Santa Marina and Point 36. Some confusion would later arise about the Buffs' involvement.

At about 0630hrs, Lt. Col. B. D. Tarleton, commanding the Royal West Kents, arrived by jeep at Fortress Headquarters for a briefing by Tilney. Tarleton could hardly have welcomed having to send his men into the fray so soon after their arrival, or be pleased to learn that, during the attack, A Company was to be directed by the brigadier from a vantage point atop Meraviglia. He would surely have been even less impressed had he known about the previous day's failed attempt to secure Point 100. Nor was he told that, because of the already overloaded wireless net, communication between Fortress Headquarters and A Company was to be by runner. Owing to the confused situation, there would be no pre-arranged artillery bombardment. Instead, artillery and machine guns were to stand by to support A Company as required.

Even as the British finalized their battle preparations, another offensive was under way as Kampfgruppe Dörr and the *Küstenjäger* made a renewed effort to take Pandeli castle. It failed owing to a concerted effort by the guns on and around Mounts Vigla, Meraviglia and della Palma.

At 0830hrs, A Company crossed its attack start line. As usual, Ju 87 Stukas were overhead. From 0900hrs dive-bombing attacks intensified, resulting in casualties among personnel of Battalion Headquarters of the Royal West Kents at Charing Cross. In addition to aerial bombing, Meraviglia was constantly swept with machine-gun and cannon fire. For a while, German mortars firing from Point 100 fell around the area of Brigade Headquarters.

From the northern slopes of Meraviglia, the Faughs targeted German forces on Rachi with machine guns and mortars. The 25-pdr field guns added to the destruction, concentrating in particular on German positions at P.L. 211 near the northern end of Rachi.

As soon as the leading platoons of A Company were past Searchlight Hill, they were bombed by Stukas and subjected to sniper and mortar fire. The attack continued, meeting automatic fire from Point 100 and P.L. 211. With the King's Own and the Faughs providing fire support, small groups moved from cover to cover. They fought their way to within 50 yards of the German positions, before having to withdraw and re-organize in dead ground south-east of Searchlight Hill. There were many casualties. Major Butler had been lightly wounded but remained in command and prepared for a second attempt to take the enemy positions.

Owing to communication problems, a runner had in the meantime been sent from Battalion Headquarters of the Royal West Kents with a reminder for C Company not to attack until ordered. The runner returned to report that the OC, Maj. M. R. Read, had acted on his initiative and, contrary to orders, was already occupying Santa Marina. When he was informed of the progress made by Read, the brigadier sent word that C Company was to halt its advance immediately. He then decided to proceed with the rest of his plan, regardless of whether or not Point 100 could be taken. While Tilney was giving his orders, a message arrived informing him of the failed attack by A Company, with a request by Butler for close mortar support and smoke from the 25-pdrs for a renewed effort at 1430hrs. This was agreed.

With a stream of constant interruptions, the O Group dragged on for two hours. As a newcomer to Leros, Tarleton was able to observe events from a unique perspective. He had been shipped from a comparatively tranquil and orderly setting and pitched into a desperate and chaotic battle. He listened, as Tilney altered the objective of C Company which was now instructed to take not just Point 36, but to push on to the road junction of San Nicola and Villa Belleni. Supporting fire was to be provided by mortars and medium machine guns of the Faughs and all available coastal batteries and 25-pdrs. The CO of the Faughs, Maj. Shephard, was tasked with organizing a composite company to be sent to Santa Marina to follow C Company and mop up pockets of resistance. Shephard was doubtful whether he could find sufficient men in the time available. Tarleton, too, expressed misgivings, arguing that the forces available were hardly sufficient for the task ahead. Tilney concurred, but was not dissuaded. H-Hour was fixed for 1500hrs.

Tarleton made his way to C Company's location south of Platanos, arriving there ahead of the runner from Fortress Headquarters. With 15 minutes to spare, the CO was able to prevent Read from continuing towards Point 36 – and into supporting fire scheduled for the same time. As there was no sign of the expected Faughs, Tarleton reluctantly postponed H-Hour until 1530hrs, too late for those who would be attacking to benefit from the pre-arranged fire plan.

The second attack along Rachi had commenced at 1425hrs. Following the same route as before, it was made by two composite platoons led by Maj. Butler and the company 2 i/c, Capt. William Grimshaw. All available light machine guns were grouped alongside Searchlight Hill under Lt. H. D. T. Groom (who had been wounded) and an officer of the King's Own. Smoke was laid over enemy positions, with mortar support provided by a detachment of the Faughs. The Germans responded with automatic and

Atop Point 204 (Meraviglia) was an Italian battery (P.L. 127) comprising six 90/53 dual-purpose guns. Fortress HQ was established in a tunnel that ran through the hilltop, with an entrance/exit at both ends and a vertical shaft providing access to an observation post. This is the so-called western entrance/exit, where Brig. Tilney was taken prisoner on 16 November. (Author's collection)

mortar fire, and the King's Own officer with Groom's party was killed almost immediately. The attack was already under way when two sections of 14 Platoon (Royal West Kents) arrived in the Searchlight Hill area, having gone astray while moving up for the assault on Point 36. Mistaking them for reinforcements, Groom directed the soldiers forward against Point 100.

By this time, all that could be mustered of the Faughs to support the attack by C Company of the Royal West Kents were approximately 60 of all ranks remaining from B and C Companies and 17 Platoon of D Company. Ten minutes before H-Hour, two officers and 19 men arrived (probably Capt. J. W. Salter and Lt. J. Duffy with B Company) and informed Tarleton that a similar number were also on the way. Orders were given during an ongoing aerial bombardment. At 1525hrs, Tilney appeared and demanded to know what the delay was. The attack began five minutes later.

On the right was 13 Platoon, with the Faughs behind. To compensate for the two sections now fighting on Rachi, a patrol team from Company Headquarters and one section from the reserve platoon of C Company were attached to 14 Platoon on the left. 15 Platoon (less one section) was reserve, followed closely by the battalion R Group, (Reconnaissance Group) comprising four ORs and two officers including Tarleton. Major Read and a runner were positioned between the two forward platoons, with the company 2 i/c Capt. E. E. Newbald, and Company Headquarters behind. The advance began as intended, but for 14 Platoon again moving too far west and ending up on Searchlight Hill. On this occasion, the men were led from the area, and out of the battle by the platoon commander, Lt. Richard Norris. Lower down, Read was seriously wounded after being shot in the shoulder. Command of the company passed to Eddie Newbald. When Lt. Jode of 13 Platoon was wounded, Sgt. Wallington assumed command and took charge of clearing Krithoni. German machine-gunners and riflemen covered the area from high ground and snipers concentrated on individual soldiers. Each and every building was a potential enemy strongpoint. Whenever they advanced, the troops risked being attacked by Stukas, whose pilots were directed by spotters firing red signal lights.

Meanwhile, Lt. Ted Johnson, commanding C Company of the Faughs, had reached Platanos with no more than 16 men. There, Lt. Austin Ardill provided a cursory briefing. Johnson was told to watch for a combination of Verey lights, which would be his cue to follow up the line of advance, taking care of enemy resistance along the way. Because he arrived late, however, he was left in ignorance of their actual objectives.

Owing to the limited view of the terrain ahead, C Company Headquarters of the Royal West Kents had pressed on until it was roughly in line with 13 Platoon south-east of Point 36. The battalion R Group, having been joined by a small party of the Faughs, was established on a sunken road some 300 yards short of the main objective. 15 Platoon had swung left, level with the lead formations. At about 1615hrs, Lt. John Browne, OC 15 Platoon, was tasked with seizing Point 36. Using the cover afforded by the sunken road, his platoon hastened to the left flank of 13 Platoon. Their objective was taken, together with a number of prisoners.

The Germans were quick to react by directing mortar fire onto the feature, supported by automatic fire aimed at British and surrendering Germans alike. Point 36 was thus cleared. Among the casualties was Browne, who was shot and wounded in hand and chest.

On Rachi the Royal West Kents had persevered in their attacks on Point 100. No more than a dozen or so reached their objective. In the final assault, Capt. Grimshaw was wounded, and Maj. Butler was again shot and this time paralysed in his right leg. At dusk, 7./Gren.Rgt. 65 re-occupied Point 36, enabling German forces to regain their hold along a line south to Points 100 and 109.

At Appetici, there was a follow-up attack by German forces at 1400hrs. After fighting for more than two hours, and supported by Stukas and mortar fire, the *Küstenjäger*, 6./Lw.-Jäger-Rgt. 22 and 9./Gren.Rgt. 440 overran 9 Platoon of the Faughs and took Pandeli castle. With the enemy now in control of the Appetici castle feature, the scene was set for a link-up with Kampfgruppe von Saldern, whose forces were preparing to push east via Platanos to Pandeli for an assault on Meraviglia from the north and north-east.

It was an altogether different picture for the Royal West Kents. With the remnants of 13 and 15 Platoons scattered between the coast and Rachi, and with no sign of the whereabouts of 14 Platoon, Tarleton was unable to press on. He therefore ordered a withdrawal to the area of Battalion Headquarters – situated on a spur that ran north from the defended slopes of Meraviglia to the sea.

The anticipated push by the Buffs seems to have occurred late in the afternoon, although it is unclear which company was involved. In the event, nothing was achieved. Tarleton would later claim that he had been expecting the Buffs to put in a *battalion* attack and that Tilney had altered this aspect of the battle plan without his knowledge.

That night, as the Royal West Kents Padre, Capt. G. M. Young, assisted with the wounded, he unexpectedly encountered a column of enemy troops. The Padre was left to continue his work, and later reported having seen over a thousand lightly equipped troops pass by, all heading in the direction of Meraviglia.

In neutral waters off Turkey, shortly before 1800hrs, several MTBs each transhipped from HMS *Belvoir* 25 troops of the Royal West Kents. The remainder, including D Company, were taken on board other vessels. The faster torpedo boats reached Lakki after nearly three and a half hours. On arrival, the senior naval officer was instructed to disembark all troops and then to proceed immediately to Alinda to engage surface vessels entering the bay. Just before the MTBs got under way, the order was countermanded. Puzzled, the force commander decided to ignore instructions, and soon after 2200hrs set course for Alinda.

During the night, Battalion Headquarters of the Royal West Kents was outflanked. German troops closed to within grenade-throwing range. The Adjutant, Capt. Donald J. Cropper, ordered a withdrawal to an RV farther uphill. Before long, Cropper and Capt. C. M. Bernard were both wounded. Cropper tried to reach the Regimental Aid Post, only to be taken prisoner (he later escaped). A series of short withdrawals brought Bernard and the remnants of Battalion Headquarters, together with a few stragglers, to a machine-gun post manned by the Faughs. By now, the total strength of Bernard's party was little more than a dozen. They were spared a follow-up attack, as the intention of the Germans seems to have been to clear the way for a link-up with their comrades on Point 189.

During the afternoon, III./1.Rgt. 'Brandenburg' had assembled at Kalymnos. These final reinforcements embarked on four Pi-La-Booten and one F-lighter for passage to Leros, with orders to liaise with Kampfgruppe von Saldern and safeguard the landing of heavy weapons in Pandeli Bay. Three Flak (anti-aircraft), six Pak (anti-tank) and two light guns were loaded aboard two Pi-La-Boote, which were to follow the troop transports and stand by off Leros, beyond reach of the coastal batteries.

In order to prevent further German reinforcements from arriving by sea, HM ships *Penn*, *Aldenham* and *Blencathra* had remained at readiness in Turkish waters throughout the day. At dusk, *Blencathra* left Turk Buku to take *Rockwood* under tow to Cyprus. Later still, *Penn* was advised of enemy craft south-east of Kalymnos, steering northward for Leros (evidently the Brandenburg reinforcements). It took an hour for the information to be relayed through Alexandria. The captain of HMS *Penn*, Lt. Cdr. James Swain, decided it was then too late to act, and instead carried out previous instructions to sweep the east coast of Leros at dawn. It was a fateful decision.

Under heavy fire from coastal batteries, the first wave of landing craft with 280 men of III./1.Rgt. 'Brandenburg' reached Leros at 2140hrs, just as the port authorities at Lakki were supervising the disembarkation of the Royal West Kents. The second wave with heavy weapons remained offshore when it was realized that Pandeli Bay was not yet in German hands. The Brandenburg reinforcements came ashore on the east side of Appetici and

On 16 November, a joint Italian–British defence was conducted atop Meraviglia. Among those who distinguished themselves was Lt. Alan Phipps, RN. He was considered for an award of the Victoria Cross but, because of a lack of eyewitnesses, instead received a Posthumous Mention in Dispatches. Almost certainly, Phipps was originally buried in this communal grave below No. 4 gun. (Author's collection)

but a short march from Pandeli town. This was reached by the point troops at the same time as those of Kampfgruppe von Saldern, subsequent to their link-up with Kampfgruppe Dörr and the Küstenjäger at Castello di Bronzi. With enemy forces massed around the north and north-eastern slopes of Meraviglia, the final phase in the battle for Leros was about to begin.

The British MTBs that had earlier left Lakki, had proceeded to Alinda. Nothing untoward was seen and so the three boats withdrew towards Kalymnos. German forces off Pandeli observed their departure, but did not intervene.

As the noose tightened around Meraviglia, Tilney issued orders for the 16th: Lt. Col. Tarleton was to direct D Company of the Royal West Kents in an attempt to secure Point 100, while B Company of the Royal West Kents along with D Company of the Buffs launched a simultaneous attack to clear San Nicola and the hospital area. As soon as Point 100 was taken, Tarleton was to take charge of all troops on Rachi and drive the enemy eastward into the sea. Tilney was interrupted by the arrival of two signallers with a situation report that had been dispatched by Capt. Cropper shortly before he was wounded. It included news of a suspected enemy landing at Alinda Bay. Tilney, who could not possibly have realized the implications of the latest events, decided that the attack on Point 100 would continue regardless. The King's Own were gathered at Searchlight Hill as support. Ted Johnson with his depleted company – now less than platoon strength – was to join A Company of the Faughs in supporting the attack against San Nicola.

The main defence of Meraviglia was dependent on two platoons of A Company situated on the spur projecting from the north-east towards Platanos, and 50 or so officers and men from Brigade under Lt. Col. C. W. M. Ritchie covering the eastern approaches. It was considered that there was little likelihood of enemy forces launching an attack from the west, which was virtually devoid of cover, and that any attempt to take the feature would come from the east. Accordingly, before midnight, Lt. Col. J. R. Easonsmith, commanding the LRDG, was ordered by Tilney to send two patrols down either side of the east face towards Platanos in order to deny the area to the enemy. Both parties ran into German troops en route to Pandeli. Jake Easonsmith was killed following which, Col. Guy Prendergast (OC Raiding Forces Aegean and LRDG former CO) reassumed command.

After dark, 177 German prisoners of war boarded an Italian F-lighter at Partheni Bay and, at Lakki, embarkation of wounded continued. Among the last to be evacuated was Maj. Robert Butler.

In the evening, the German *U-565* registered a torpedo hit on a submarine south-east of Kos; her victim was undoubtedly the British submarine *Simoon*, reported missing with all hands. Elsewhere, Allied forces achieved a minor success, when a detachment of SBS raided Symi. An ammunition dump was destroyed, the power station and several caiques were damaged, and nearly two dozen occupation troops were killed. The attackers withdrew without loss to themselves.


# 16 NOVEMBER

Lieutenant-Colonel Tarleton rejoined his battalion at the Anchor at about 0100hrs on the 16th. He deployed his men to cover likely approach routes from the north and to support any move by D Company. Lieutenant Richard

From the photograph album of Walter Keller (front), a machine-gunner in 3./-Fallschirmjäger-Rgt. 2, dated 17 November and captioned: After the battle with Piepl Monska. (Author's collection)

Norris was ordered to take his platoon to a road 500 yards north-east of its present location. Accounting for the possibility that D Company's task was liable to change, Tarleton took the added precaution of placing his newly arrived troops in deep Italian trenches east of the Anchor road junction, which afforded some cover from air attack while enabling them to counter any threat from the direction of Appetici. The Mortar Platoon was sited to cover the approaches from Platanos and Appetici and to support D Company as required. The Anti-Aircraft (AA) Platoon under Capt. M. B. Rickcord was tasked with moving as a fighting patrol along the road to Alinda Bay, to contact any members of the battalion en route, and to watch for and report any signs of enemy movement south. Rickcord returned at 0445hrs, having lost three men who had been wounded when they entered an Italian minefield. No British troops other than Lt. Norris's platoon had been encountered, and no Germans were observed in Platanos.

All German units on Leros had now been placed under the command of Maj. von Saldern. Before dawn, German forces launched a major assault along the northern face of Meraviglia. At about 0515hrs, Tarleton was informed that Norris was dead and his platoon had been driven back towards the Anchor. Moreover, the enemy had reached the commanding south-eastern spur of Meraviglia.

In an effort to counter the threat, Tarleton immediately re-deployed Rickcord's Platoon. He also telephoned Fortress Headquarters with a situation report, only to be told by the brigade Intelligence officer that there was no cause for concern, as an operation was already under way to clear the ridge. (At some point during the morning, Tilney had sent for 160 men gathered at Lakki to help defend Meraviglia.) Tarleton asked to speak to the brigadier and suggested that, in view of developments, D Company's task be changed. But Tilney refused to alter his plan.

Meanwhile, Rickcord and his men pressed on in the face of constant enemy fire. Eventually, a route was found west of the Anchor that enabled the leading elements to approach to within 250 yards of Germans on the summit.

During the night, there had been an attempt to gather at the Anchor scattered personnel of C Company of the Royal West Kents. A composite platoon was formed under Capt. Newbald and directed to take up a defensive position behind that of D Company. At about the same time, a message was received by Capt. C. M. Bernard instructing D Company not to move and requesting the company commander, Maj. Anthony J. M. Flint, to call Fortress Headquarters. The information was dispatched to Flint, but never reached him. Neither was Tarleton kept informed. Unaware of the change of plan, Tarleton and Flint left by jeep at about 0700hrs to reconnoitre the ground for D Company's attack. With daylight, the Luftwaffe had returned and the vehicle made an easy target. The jeep was abandoned. On the eastern heights of Meraviglia there was increasingly heavier firing and aircraft were seen wheeling and diving over the south-eastern slopes. Fearing a major assault on the Anchor, Tarleton decided to return with his party on foot.

In fact, the focus of attention was Meraviglia. Atop the feature, Ritchie had rounded up two Royal Signals officers, Capt. Ramsay and Lt. E. B. Horton, with half a dozen men having taken up positions in and around the battery command post. Under constant machine-gun and sniper fire from the castle area 1,000 yards (nearly a kilometre) away, the party watched and waited. Half an hour passed before the first Germans were seen approaching. Ritchie fired and the group – about 12 strong – went to ground. Two more Germans were observed about 130 yards away. Ritchie shot them both.

Owing to the precarious situation, Tilney decided to evacuate his own and LRDG Headquarters and to relocate to Lakki. To prevent their being captured and compromised, secret ciphers were destroyed. At 0825hrs the Germans intercepted a signal from Fortress Headquarters to General Headquarters (GHQ) in Cairo. It advised that the situation was critical; enemy forces supported by Stukas and machine-gun fire were reinforcing the Leros peninsula, and defensive positions on Meraviglia had been neutralized leaving troops demoralized and facing a hopeless situation. When the message was translated and relayed to Kampfgruppe Müller, it was duplicated in leaflet form with additional words of encouragement from the German commander: 'It is time to finish off the enemy!' Copies were

After the battle, *Fallschirmjäger* help themselves to bottles of Chianti. This building, just inland of Alinda Bay, later became the hotel Archontiko Angelou. (Author's collection)

then dropped over German positions by Arado floatplanes. Müller knew he was close to victory. The source of the signal, apparently sent in plain language, is a mystery. But for the Germans, it was an unexpected and welcome bonus and exactly what was required to boost the morale of their own forces.

Before Fortress Headquarters was evacuated, Maj. H. E. Scott, OC HQ Company of the Royal West Kents, received a telephone message from Tilney ordering D Company to attack north along the Porta Vecchia–Platanos road with the intention of pushing the enemy back into the sea. A written message was sent to the OC of D Company, but there is no record of it reaching its destination. In any event, Tilney himself arrived soon after and reaffirmed the order, to the consternation of the company 2 i/c, Capt. P. R. H. Turner, for any movement along the road was met with an immediate response from the Germans on the commanding heights.

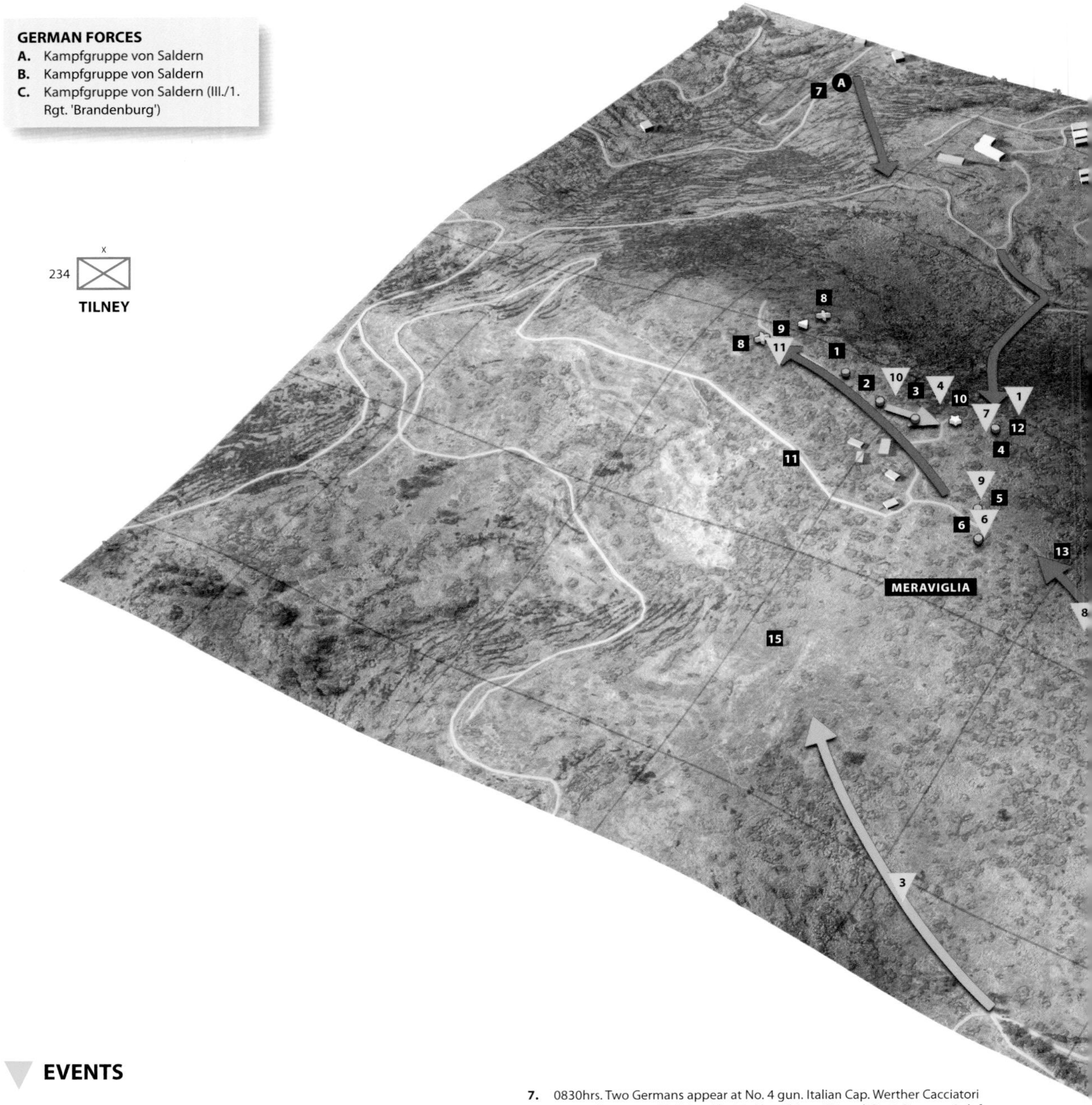
GERMAN FORCES
A. Kampfgruppe von Saldern
B. Kampfgruppe von Saldern
C. Kampfgruppe von Saldern (III./1. Rgt. 'Brandenburg')
234
TILNEY
MERAVIGLIA

## EVENTS

1. 0300hrs. One German prisoner is taken by the Royal Irish Fusiliers at an outpost on the north-eastern spur of Meraviglia.

2. 0615hrs. German forces approach along the eastern spur of Meraviglia.

3. Captain Rickcord (Royal West Kents) and the AA Platoon reach partway up the southern side of Meraviglia but the group becomes separated. Rickcord with two sections joins forces with the Royal Irish Fusiliers in defending the area.

4. 0715hrs. Lieutenant-Colonel Ritchie (G1 at Brigade HQ) together with Capt. Ramsay (Bde Signals Officer) and Capt. Horton (Royal Signals) take up position with six men in and around the battery command post. Firing towards the east and north-east indicates the progress of German forces.

5. 0745hrs. German soldiers are observed at the Breda HMG position on the eastern spur of the height, defended by a party under Capt. Wood. This prompts a withdrawal by Capt. Gibbon, situated slightly further uphill.

6. 0815hrs. Two German soldiers are shot when they appear just 130 yards south-east of the battery CP, heading towards Nos. 5 and 6 guns.

7. 0830hrs. Two Germans appear at No. 4 gun. Italian Cap. Werther Cacciatori requests assistance and is joined by Lt. Alan Phipps RN and Capt. Ramsay. A defence by Italian and British forces is conducted at the gun position. Lieutenant Phipps is killed and Cap. Cacciatori seriously wounded.

8. 0945–1015hrs. German forces (probably III./1. 'Brandenburg') continue to appear in the vicinity of the Breda HMG position, heading towards Nos. 5 and 6 guns positions 5 and 6.

9. 1045hrs. A white flag appears in the vicinity of Nos. 5 and 6 guns. About five minutes later, those at the battery CP withdraw to the area of No. 2 gun.

10. At 1130hrs, Lt. Col. Ritchie, together with Maj. Dixon (Cheshire Regt), Capt. Duncan (RA) and about 12 ORs, counter-attacks with the intention of reclaiming the battery CP and Nos. 5 and 6 guns. The battery CP is reoccupied, but Ritchie is wounded. At some point, both Dixon and Duncan are killed. Colonel Prendergast (LRDG) takes charge of the defence.

11. 1630hrs. After a respite of several hours, German forces launch a renewed effort to take the height. 9. Kompanie of III./1. 'Brandenburg' closes in on Fortress HQ and Brig. Tilney and his staff are taken prisoner.

# MERAVIGLIA, 16 NOVEMBER 1943

Final phase of battle: Fortress Headquarters overrun by German forces

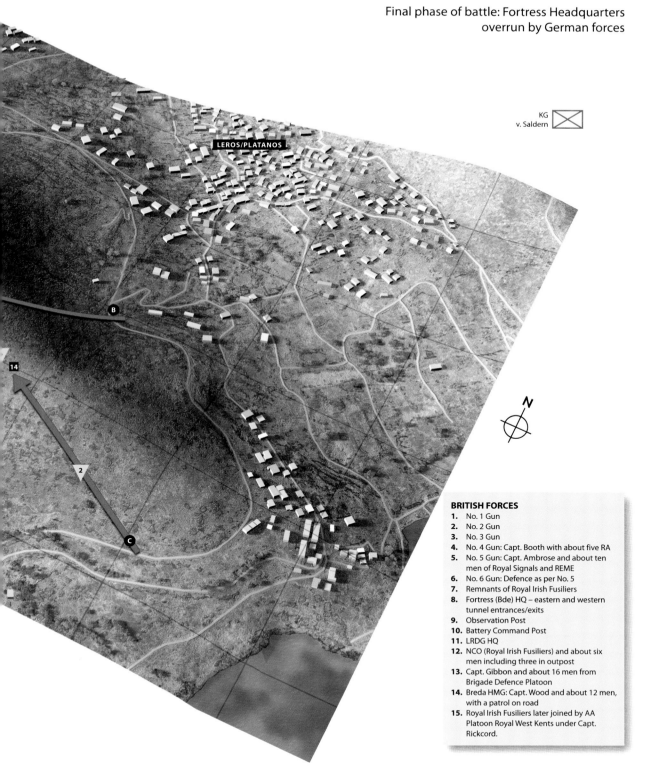

KG
v. Saldern

LEROS/PLATANOS

**BRITISH FORCES**

1. No. 1 Gun
2. No. 2 Gun
3. No. 3 Gun
4. No. 4 Gun: Capt. Booth with about five RA
5. No. 5 Gun: Capt. Ambrose and about ten men of Royal Signals and REME
6. No. 6 Gun: Defence as per No. 5
7. Remnants of Royal Irish Fusiliers
8. Fortress (Bde) HQ – eastern and western tunnel entrances/exits
9. Observation Post
10. Battery Command Post
11. LRDG HQ
12. NCO (Royal Irish Fusiliers) and about six men including three in outpost
13. Capt. Gibbon and about 16 men from Brigade Defence Platoon
14. Breda HMG: Capt. Wood and about 12 men, with a patrol on road
15. Royal Irish Fusiliers later joined by AA Platoon Royal West Kents under Capt. Rickcord.

At about 0830hrs, Tarleton arrived back at the Anchor to a scene of disarray, with the area under small arms and mortar fire and aerial attack. To the north-west, the AA Platoon was attempting to reach the top of Meraviglia, with supporting fire provided by the battalion's mortars. Through the dust and smoke, German snipers could be seen moving among the boulders and scrub on Meraviglia's slopes. They were engaged from north-west of the Anchor by troops posted as local defence for Battalion Headquarters. With movement becoming increasingly difficult, C Company, together with 18 Platoon D Company, was repositioned slightly farther west.

Tarleton was not informed about Tilney's earlier visit nor did he realize that Fortress Headquarters had been evacuated or that D Company had been re-tasked. Neither was he aware of any orders already given to Turner. The brigadier, who had remained in the vicinity rather than proceeding to Lakki as originally planned, sought out Tarleton later in the morning and updated him on developments. The battalion commander was dismayed to learn of the brigadier's latest intentions for D Company. While Tarleton tried to dissuade the brigadier, a telephone link was established with Col. Prendergast, who had returned to Fortress Headquarters to see if the wireless sets there could be relocated to Lakki. The interruption saved D Company from almost certain annihilation and convinced Tilney that he should return to Meraviglia and continue to try and direct the battle from there.

While Tilney was speaking with Prendergast, Tarleton noticed men doubling south-west from D Company's location. He alerted Maj. Gavin Shaw, who was nearby. The 2 i/c left, saying 'I'll fix it.' Possibly, the movement was D Company forming up for the attack under Capt. Turner (who would have been acting on Tilney's orders independently and of whose instructions neither Tarleton nor Shaw were aware). Arriving at D Company's rear area, Shaw tried to determine what was happening. He looked around a wall, was hit by small arms fire in the thigh and forearm, and died soon afterwards.

Ritchie, together with pockets of resistance, both British and Italian, had remained in contact with enemy forces throughout the morning. Owing to the initiative and courage of such individuals, Tilney was able to return to Meraviglia. Before doing so, he ordered Tarleton to muster his available forces and to advance northward via the western slopes of Rachi Ridge and establish contact with the Buffs. Tarleton was to place his men under command of Lt. Col. Iggulden, whereupon the combined force was to attack south via Rachi and concentrate on Meraviglia. Tarleton made his way to Battalion Headquarters. He at once clarified the situation: cancelling the proposed attack by D Company, and informing Turner of the latest plan. Mortars were disabled and extra bandoliers of small arms ammunitions issued. Efforts to contact the AA Platoon were unsuccessful. It seems that two of the sections tried, and failed, to rejoin the battalion, whereas the remaining two sections under Capt. Rickcord remained in action on Meraviglia until the very end.

Earlier that morning, Lt. Ted Johnson had redeployed his men on the lower slopes of Rachi/Meraviglia to cover the proposed attack on San Nicola. When this failed to materialize, Johnson found himself trapped in an increasingly precarious position where the slightest movement brought an instant response from enemy positions lower down. In order to stay awake Johnson had been taking the amphetamine Benzedrine. But as the effect wore off, he was overcome with exhaustion and unable to think clearly. With

Hauptmann Helmut Dörr (looking directly at camera) at an assembly area for British prisoners of war, most or all of them NCOs and WOs. (BA: 101I-528-2356-34)

Johnson was Lt. Tom Massey-Lynch (A Company) and three or four soldiers. A decision was made to destroy what equipment they could, after which the party reluctantly surrendered.

In the neighbourhood of San Nicola, the Buffs and B Company of the Royal West Kents had returned to the previous day's positions and taken over from the LRDG patrols after an uneventful night. The day dawned with none of the usual signs of enemy movement, prompting Capt. Flood, OC B Company, to send Lieutenants Caller and Gordon Huckle on a reconnaissance into San Nicola. When it was discovered that the Germans had abandoned the area, the company pushed forward on to Point 100 and Rachi Ridge, with D Company of the Buffs advancing on their left. Only a small number of individual Germans were found in dugouts. By 1030hrs, B Company of the Royal West Kents had established contact with the King's Own on Searchlight Hill. Captain Flood, Lt. Col. Egerton of the King's Own, and Maj. E. W. Tassell, commanding D Company of the Buffs, gathered for an impromptu conference, after which Tassell left to report to his CO. At about 1130hrs, Egerton told Flood that, as a result of what had been observed in the area of Fortress Headquarters, he was withdrawing all troops from the Rachi feature to join up with the Buffs at the north end of the island. B Company was instructed to cover the withdrawal. Subsequently, Egerton, Tassell and Flood were reunited on the north-western outskirts of San Nicola, where they encountered a none-too-pleased Lt. Col. Iggulden.

In the meantime, the Royal West Kents in the Anchor area – about 160 all ranks – were on the move. It is never easy to disengage and withdraw when in contact with the enemy in daylight. To minimize losses, the Royal West Kents headed south-west and into cover before moving northward in the general direction of San Giovanni. Although the troops were harassed by small arms fire, there was no follow-up by German ground forces. But as soon as it was vacated, the battalion area was heavily bombed. It was probably assumed that the British were making for Lakki, as the road to the port was also bombed. Soon afterwards the port area was targeted. Large numbers of aircraft remained overhead throughout the rest of the morning and into the afternoon, but fortunately for the infantry the Luftwaffe seemed more interested in the gun positions in the area of Mounts Patella and San Giovanni.

The Royal West Kents had to negotiate terrain that is rough and undulating and intersected by ravines. Bordering the ravines and on the lower hill slopes, olive groves and terraced fields afforded a certain amount of cover, but higher up the vegetation is generally sparse, consisting mainly of the ubiquitous Greek spiny spurge. Progress was hindered by long-range sniper fire. Along the way, small parties from different units were encountered; some heading for pre-arranged RVs, others making for the beaches, but all moving away from Meraviglia and the enemy. It was evident that command had completely broken down and there was little hope of organizing an effective counter-attack. Nevertheless, Tarleton pressed on and at around 1300hrs, Battalion Headquarters reached the heights north-east of San Giovanni, overlooking Gurna Bay. An hour later, Capt. Mike Rochford turned up with written confirmation of Tilney's morning orders, for forwarding to Iggulden. It was assumed that Point 100 and San Nicola were still strongly defended by the enemy. No one seemed sure about Meraviglia anymore. Under the circumstances it was decided to skirt around the south side of Rachi to try to reach the Buffs by moving south and west of Germano, using the cover afforded by broken ground at the base of the feature. Sub-unit RVs were allocated close to Point 177 (Condrida) and, it was hoped, not far from where the Buffs were.

At Meraviglia, Ritchie had continued to hold on. When, on the south-eastern edge of the height, No. 5 and 6 guns were overrun, there was little to prevent the Germans from reaching Fortress Headquarters. Ritchie ordered his party to fall back to where they could best cover the plateau and the eastern approaches of the headquarters tunnel. He was joined by Maj. Richard H. Dixon of the Cheshire Regiment, together with Capt. Charles S. Duncan, Royal Artillery, and about a dozen troops. During a counter-attack, Ritchie was wounded. Shortly afterwards, Dixon was shot dead. But the German assault had lost its momentum and, for a while, the situation was stabilized, with Prendergast having been assigned by Tilney to take charge of the defence.

Members of the defeated Leros garrison on their way to Portolago and a transport vessel to the mainland. Note the camouflage-painted helmets, which were unique to Malta-based units. (Dr. med. Georg Repp via Verena Repp-Gröpl)

After having recently returned to Meraviglia, at about 1245hrs, Tilney again left by jeep to find and brief Egerton and to reconnoitre Rachi Ridge. Searchlight Hill and Point 109 appeared to be deserted, and there was no sign of movement by the Royal West Kents along the western slopes. Eventually, the brigadier found two men of the King's Own, and learned that, in view of the deteriorating situation, their CO had ordered a general withdrawal north. It was apparent that Tarleton could not be expected to RV with the Buffs in time to organize a joint defence about

Meraviglia. Tilney therefore amended his plan and sent the two soldiers by jeep with instructions for Tarleton to concentrate his force in the area of Porta Vecchia. The message never got through, and Tilney and Tarleton were to stay out of touch for the remainder of the battle. Tilney's next move was to seek out the Buffs and re-deploy them on Meraviglia. Iggulden was located, in discussion with Tarleton and Lt. Cdr. Frank Ramseyer. Tilney placed Tarleton under the command of Iggulden, who was also instructed to round up the many stragglers now making their way from the battle area towards Partheni. With so many troops concentrated in one place, San Nicola had become a prime target for the Luftwaffe. Tilney instructed Iggulden to send one company to reinforce by dusk the scattered troops still on Meraviglia, with the remainder to follow under cover of darkness.

Tilney was unaware that the majority of the Royal West Kents were then only a short distance away, still heading towards San Nicola. B Echelon had gone ahead to try to contact the Buffs, leaving C Company to lead the way through the vegetation and trees below Rachi's southern slopes. HQ Company, Battalion Headquarters and D Company followed at ten-minute intervals. En route, caves and tunnels were checked lest they concealed the enemy. More often than not, they were found to harbour Italians and stragglers from other units. It was a time-consuming process accompanied by much shouting and movement and before long it attracted fire from Point 100. Either the Germans had never relinquished possession of the feature, or else had filtered back during the day. From Rachi, signal lights were fired to indicate the position of the Royal West Kents. Moments later, aircraft carried out a low-level sweep, but left after only a superficial search. The troops continued towards the Germano–Condrida area where they took up defensive positions.

The precise location of the Buffs was still unknown and Tarleton did not want to risk travelling at night in unfamiliar terrain. With evening approaching, he therefore dispatched a search patrol under Lt. J. A. Myers. He returned at about 2200hrs with a written message from the Buffs second-in-command, Maj. D. B. Pyke: The Buffs, together with all other troops in the locality, had been ordered south to Meraviglia, and Pyke was en route with a rear party to the San Giovanni area. To Tarleton's surprise, Pyke made no mention of the arrival and role of the Royal West Kents. Tarleton, of course, had not received word that Tilney had revised his decision to send the battalion north. Tarleton decided to stay where he was until daybreak, unaware, as was Iggulden, that the outcome of the battle had already been decided.

The situation was no less confusing for those farther south. Earlier in the day, Lt. Clifford Clark with his party had rounded up many who were fleeing from Meraviglia. Shortly afterwards, Clark was contacted by an officer with orders from Tilney for all troops to RV at the Anchor, preparatory to launching a counter-attack to recapture Meraviglia. Clark therefore withdrew his force from San Giovanni. After a slow and hazardous journey under continual air attack, Clark reached the outskirts of Lakki. A patrol was sent to reconnoitre the Anchor, and the remaining troops were deployed under cover while Clark continued to the port headquarters to enquire about the situation. No one there seemed to know what was happening. Clark decided to return to San Giovanni, collecting stragglers along the way. Midway through the journey, word was received that Brig. Tilney had capitulated.

Tilney had returned to Meraviglia and disappointing news that the expected 160 reinforcements from Lakki had failed to materialize. An officer was therefore sent to hasten the arrival of the Buffs' advance company. Like so many others, the message never arrived. At the same time, word was received from GHQ that the Aegean was to be evacuated the following night. Further details were to follow, but if there was a follow-up signal, it was sent too late to have any effect. (Earlier in the day, the Navy had, in fact, received instructions to collect all small craft at Turk Buku under orders of the British destroyer *Fury* – which had arrived in the area with HMS *Exmoor* and the Polish *Krakowiak* – in preparation for a possible evacuation of Leros.) Colonel Prendergast was dispatched to Lakki to fetch whoever he could for a counter-attack. He had no sooner left, than mortar, machine-gun and small arms fire intensified as the enemy launched the final assault on Meraviglia. It became impossible to leave Fortress Headquarters by the east exit. Before long, troops from III./1.Rgt. 'Brandenburg' were also covering the west entrance. Realizing there was nothing more he could do, Tilney sent a man who could speak German to parley with the enemy. Before he could make himself understood, however, he was shot and wounded. When the Germans were made aware of the situation, those inside the tunnel were allowed to emerge. It was 1630hrs. Meraviglia had been overrun by units of II./Gren.Rgt. 65, II./Gren.Rgt. 16 and III./1.Rgt. 'Brandenburg' – the latter under Oblt. Max Wandrey following the wounding earlier in the day of the battalion commander, Hptm. Gustav Fröböse. Brigadier Tilney had no desire to prolong the inevitable. Suddenly, the battle for Leros was over.

The task now facing the Germans was how to convince the garrison that Tilney had surrendered. A bizarre situation unfolded as British officers and their captors travelled together in jeeps to locate the many scattered units still holding out. Disbelieving troops were informed of Tilney's decision, and ordered to lay down their arms. The brigadier and the Senior British Naval Officer, Capt. Edmund H. D. Baker, RN, were escorted by two German officers and driven to Lakki to co-ordinate the surrender with Contramm. Luigi Mascherpa. Signals were also sent advising Italian and British command of events. Generalleutnant Müller was at sea en route to Leros when news of the surrender reached him. Initially, he was dubious, failing to understand how a commander could continue to have any influence over his forces when he was a prisoner of war. Müller landed at Castello di Bronzi at 2130hrs and was assured by Maj. von Saldern personally that the garrison had indeed capitulated.

As the final moments of the battle were being played out, Beaufighters had continued to operate out of sight of those on the ground, destroying a Siebel ferry west of Kalymnos. Evidently unaware of the island's surrender, after dark 216 Squadron flew 12 supply sorties to Leros, resulting in the loss of one Dakota (the crew and dispatchers survived). Throughout the five-day battle, nine Beaufighters, operating out of sight of those on the ground, had been lost, together with most of the aircrew. At least 11 German aircraft had also been written off and a number of aircrew killed or wounded.

Dawn on Wednesday, 17 November, was in stark contrast to previous days. There was virtually no gunfire. Instead, German troops could be heard happily singing their national anthem. It made little sense to those who were as yet unaware of the situation. The sense of unreality was heightened by the arrival of German seaplanes, which alighted unimpeded in Lakki Bay. The victors could hardly believe their good fortune. For those who awoke as prisoners of war, it was altogether different. Many, on learning that the fighting was over, had simply lain down and slept. Having had a few hours to recover from their exhaustion, they now faced the shocking reality of spending the rest of the war in captivity.

Only the SBS and LRDG appear to have formulated contingency plans to enable a getaway. Jellicoe and Ramseyer rounded up some 90 personnel who boarded a caique and a motorboat and before dawn on the 17th departed Leros for Turkish waters. For most, however, there was to be no escape. Approximately 3,000 British and, according to German statistics, 5,350 Italians were taken prisoner on Leros.

The last major island, Samos, was occupied by German forces without resistance on 22 November 1943.

Recognition for the victors: At Lamia in January 1944, Oberleutnant Max Wandrey (who took over command on Leros of III./1.Rgt. 'Brandenburg') receives the Knight's Cross from Regimentskommandeur, Oberstleutnant Uwe Walther. In attendance is General der Flieger Hellmuth Felmy commanding LXVIII. Armeekorps. (Author's collection)

# AFTERMATH

What became of officers who were central figures in Aegean operations? Generaloberst Alexander Löhr, V.Adm. Werner Lange, Gen.d.Fl. Martin Fiebig, and Generallt. Friedrich-Wilhelm Müller survived the war, as did the officers who commanded German battle groups during operations *Eisbär* and *Taifun*.

Löhr and Fiebig, however, were imprisoned in Yugoslavia before being sentenced to death for alleged war crimes. They were executed in 1947. Müller was taken prisoner by the Soviets in East Prussia in 1945. He was turned over to the Greeks and also tried for war crimes. Friedrich-Wilhelm Müller was found guilty and shot by firing squad on 20 May 1947, the anniversary of the German invasion of Crete. He is interred at Dionyssos-Rapendoza, in Greece, together with those who lost their lives while serving under his command during the battles for Kos and Leros.

On the British side, Lt. Gen. Sir Desmond Anderson, Col. Lionel Kenyon, Adm. Sir John Cunningham, V.Adm. Sir Algernon Willis, A.C. W. H. Dunn, A.V.M. Richard Saul and Maj. Gen. H. R. Hall survived, as did four battalion commanders: Lieutenant-Colonels Robert Kirby, Douglas Iggulden, Ben Tarleton and Egerton, together with Lord Jellicoe.

A good number of determined individuals succeeded in escaping from Kos and Leros. One group of six included two LRDG officers: New Zealander, 2Lt. R. F. White and Greek 2Lt. G. V. 'Pav' Pavlides. The latter is seen with thumbs up at Farmakonisi, en route to Turkey, on 17 November. (Author's collection)

Following his departure from Leros, 'Ben' Brittorous returned to England, where he took charge of a Home Guard unit. He retired as a Brigadier in 1946. His successor on Leros, Brig. 'Dolly' Tilney, spent nearly 18 months in German captivity before being freed by advancing American forces. He retired from the army shortly after returning to England.

Italian officers were altogether less fortunate. Shortly after the battle of Kos, an unidentified German unit was tasked with executing captured pro-Badoglio Italian officers. Among those shot was Col. Felice Leggio. Naval officers, Amm. Inigo Campioni and Contramm. Luigi Mascherpa were handed over by the Germans to authorities in the Italian Social Republic. They were sentenced to death by Special Tribunal, and executed by firing squad on 24 May 1944 in Parma.

For Britain, the Dodecanese was something that was best forgotten. An ill-conceived operation had achieved little, other than a diversion of limited German resources, but at a heavy price in human lives and *matériel*. The New Zealand government was especially scathing about the misuse of its countrymen in the LRDG. Soon afterwards, New Zealanders were withdrawn from LRDG service and on 31 December 1943, the New Zealand Squadron was disbanded altogether.

End of the line for most of the Leros garrison: Lieutenant Ted Johnson of The Royal Irish Fusiliers as a prisoner of war at Oflag VIIIF near Märisch Trübau in Sudetenland (present-day Czech Republic). (Author's collection)

Had Winston Churchill not intervened in the Dodecanese, for how long might Adolf Hitler have considered it worthwhile to retain a hold in the region? As it was, Kos and Leros remained under German occupation until the end of the war, a posting for non-effective garrison units. Crete, at the southern end of the Aegean, acquired at heavy cost in May 1941, also remained in German hands.

Events in autumn 1943 had given birth to the Allies' Raiding Forces, which went on to carry out nearly 400 hit-and-run raids on 70 islands in the Aegean. Such activities had an undeniable nuisance value and perhaps justified the continued presence in the Aegean of Axis forces. For their part, Brandenburg Küstenjäger also conducted clandestine operations. A company was based on Rhodes, another well-defended German outpost.

For Germany, the Dodecanese would represent one final, enduring, but ultimately pointless victory. As the war in mainland Europe gathered momentum, the Aegean was soon forgotten.

# THE BATTLEFIELDS TODAY

The period of Italian rule and, to a degree, World War II, have left their mark throughout the Dodecanese, especially in those islands least affected by tourism. On Kos, for example, the Italian influence is reflected in the architecture, with little to remind one about the 1943 German invasion.

Leros is different. As a less popular tourist destination, it has remained relatively unspoiled and 75 years after the battle there is still much to see. Because of its proximity to Turkey, there is on Leros a noticeable military presence. Certain areas are off limits, such as the summit of Clidi, the original Italian battery command post and surroundings having been repaired and adapted for use by the Greek armed forces.

Live ordnance is scattered throughout Leros. This 3-inch British mortar bomb was found on Point 95 in the area of Palma Bay, where a decisive encounter took place between two platoons of 5./Gren.Rgt. 65 and 18 Platoon D Company of the Buffs. (Author's collection)

Elsewhere, there are easily accessible gun positions, albeit in a much damaged state. This is due not so much to the attentions of the Luftwaffe, but as a result of post-war demolitions. Italian underground installations tend to be in good condition. However, the former headquarters tunnel inside the Greek military zone of Meraviglia is less than safe following a controlled explosion in 2018, which resulted in a partial cave-in. In residential areas there are ruins and buildings pockmarked by bullets and scarred by shrapnel. There are also fine examples of Italian military architecture, some containing murals created by bored German occupation troops.

Much of the countryside where the fighting took place is unchanged. As recently as 2014, a Bren light machine gun still in working order was discovered in the vicinity of San Giovanni – formerly the windmill feature. The Bren and many other wartime artefacts are on display at a private museum established by the late Giannis Paraponiaris and his son, Thanasis, close to the family home near the chapel of Agia Irini, in the low ground just south of Meraviglia. Another private collection may be viewed at the Hotel Elefteria in Platanos. There is also a war museum at Lakki and a small display of wartime artefacts at Villa Bellini, on the west shore of Alinda Bay.

# FURTHER READING

## Magazines and Periodicals

Drinkwater, William J., 'War in the Eastern Aegean, Part 3. The Agony of Leros' in *The Military Chest* Vol. 3, No. 5, Picton Publishing, Chippenham (1984)

Lucas, James, 'Strike on Leros' in *The Elite* Vol. 3, Issue 36, Orbis Publishing Limited (1985)

Packer, Edwin, 'Hard Lesson in the Aegean, Dodecanese Islands, Greece, September/November 1943' in *Purnell's History of the Second World War* No. 52, BPC Publishing Ltd (1975)

Pitt, Barrie, 'Into the Iron Ring' in *The Elite* Vol. 10, Issue 117, Orbis Publishing Limited (1987)

Schenk, Dr. Peter, 'The Battle for Leros' in *After the Battle* No. 90, Battle of Britain Prints International Ltd (1995)

Willis, Vice-Admiral Sir Algernon U., KCB, DSO, *Naval Operations in the Aegean between the 7th September, 1943 and 28th November, 1943*, published on 11 October 1948 as a supplement to *The London Gazette* of 8 October 1948

Wilson, General Sir H. Maitland, GCB, GBE, DSO, ADC, *Operations in the Middle East from 16th February, 1943, to 8th January, 1944*, published on 13 November 1946 as a supplement to *The London Gazette* of 12 November 1946

## Books

Benyon-Tinker, W. E., *Dust upon the Sea*, Hodder & Stoughton (1947)

Bevan, Pauline, *Travels with a Leros Veteran*, Pauline Bevan (2000)

Brandt, Günther, *Der Seekrieg in der Ägäis*, Günther Brandt (1963)

Browne, John, *Recollections of Island Warfare*, private publication

Butler, Lieutenant-Colonel Robert, MBE, MC, *Nine Lives: Through Laughing Eyes*, Invicta Publishing (1993)

Chaplin, Lieutenant-Colonel H. D., *The Queen's Own Royal West Kent Regiment 1920–1950*, Michael Joseph Ltd (1954)

Churchill, Winston S., *The Second World War: Volume V, Closing the Ring*, Cassell & Co, Ltd (1952)

Cowper, Colonel J. M., TD, *The King's Own: The Story of a Royal Regiment, Volume III. 1914–1950*, Gale & Polden Ltd (1957)

Cunliffe, Marcus, *The Royal Irish Fusiliers 1793–1950*, Oxford University Press (1952)

Gander, Leonard Marsland, *Long Road to Leros*, Macdonald & Co (1945)

Guard, J. S., *Improvise and Dare: War in the Aegean 1943–1945*, The Book Guild Ltd (1997)

Harte, Jack and Mara, Sandra, *To the Limits of Endurance: One Irishman's War*, Liberties Press (2007)

Holland, Jeffrey, *The Aegean Mission: Allied Operations in the Dodecanese, 1943*, Greenwood Press (1988)

Johnson, Edward B. W., M.C., *Island Prize: Leros, 1943*, The Kemble Press (1992)

Kay, R. L., *Long Range Desert Group in the Mediterranean*, War History Branch, Department of Internal Affairs, Wellington, New Zealand (1950)

Knight, Colonel C. R. B., OBE *Historical Records of The Buffs, Royal East Kent Regiment (3rd Foot) formerly designated The Holland Regiment and Prince George of Denmark's Regiment 1919–1948*, The Medici Society Limited (1951)

Levi, Aldo and Fioravanzo, Giuseppe, *Avvenimenti in Egeo dopo l'armistizio (Rodi, Lero e isole minori)*, Ufficio Storico della Marina Militare, Roma (1972)

Lodwick, John, *The Filibusters: The Story of The Special Boat Service*, Methuen & Co Ltd (1947)

Manicone, Gino, *I Martiri dell'Egeo: L'amaro volto di una tragedia Italiana*, Casamari (2001)

Metzsch, Friedrich-August von, *Die Geschichte der 22. I.D.*, Bad Nauheim (1952)

Nesbit, Roy C., *The Armed Rovers: Beauforts & Beaufighters over the Mediterranean*, Airlife Publishing Ltd (1995)

Pittaway, Jonathan, *Long Range Desert Group – Rhodesia*, agencies@iafrica.com

Prien, Jochen; Rodeike, Peter & Stemmer, Gerhard, *Messerschmitt Bf 109 im Einsatz bei der III. und IV./Jagdgeschwader 27, 1938–1945*, Struve-Druck (1995)

Prien, Jochen; Rodeike, Peter & Stemmer, Gerhard, *Messerschmitt Bf 109 im Einsatz bei Stab und I./Jagdgeschwader 27, 1939–1945*, Struve-Druck (1998)

Rissik, David, *The D.L.I. at War: The History of The Durham Light Infantry 1939–1945*, The Depot: The Durham Light Infantry

Rogers, Anthony, *Churchill's Folly*, Cassell (2003)

Rogers, Anthony, *Swastika over the Aegean: September–November 1943*, toro.enquiries@gmail.com (2013)

Schenk, Peter, *Kampf um die Ägäis*, Verlag E. S. Mittler & Sohn GmbH (2000)

Searle, G. W., *At Sea Level*, The Book Guild (1994)

Smith, Peter & Walker, Edwin, *War in the Aegean*, William Kimber and Co Limited (1974)

Sutherland, David, *He Who Dares: Recollections of service in the SAS, SBS and MI5*, Leo Cooper (1998)

Thompson, Julian, *The Imperial War Museum Book of War Behind Enemy Lines*, Sidgwick & Jackson published in association with the Imperial War Museum (1998)

Villa, Andrea, *Nelle isole del sole, Gli italiani nel Dodecaneso dall'occupazione al rimpatrio (1912–1947)*, Laissez-passer (2016)

Ward, S. G. P., *Faithful: The Story of the Durham Light Infantry*, Thomas Nelson & Sons Ltd

Williams, Raymond, *The Long Road from Léros*, Raymond Williams (1983)

After the war, British dead were gathered from field graves and cemeteries and reinterred in Commonwealth War Graves Commission cemeteries. This is Alinda, final resting place for 183 Allied personnel. (Author's collection)

# INDEX

Page numbers in **bold** refer to illustrations and their captions.

1st Battalion The Durham Light Infantry 12, 16, 17, 18, 26, 28–29, **30–31**, 32, 33–35

1st Battalion The King's Own Royal Regiment 12, 16, 18, 24, 58, 59, 60, 64, 66, 67, 85

II./Gren.Rgt. 16; 20, 22, 29, **30–31**, 32–33, **33**, 34, **34**, 35, 60, 71

II./Gren.Rgt. 65; **14**, 22, 28, 29, **30–31**, 32, 33–34, 35, 56–57, 58, 66, 67

II./Lw.-Jäger-Rgt. 22; 56, 58, 59, 66–67

2nd Battalion The Queen's Own Royal West Kent Regiment 12, 16, 18, 71, 72, 74–81, 84–89

2nd Battalion The Royal Irish Fusiliers (the Faughs) 12, 16, **17**, 18, 24, 57–58, 60, 62, 63–64, 67, **68–70** (70), 71, 75, 76–77, 79, 84–85

III./1.Rgt. 'Brandenburg' 78–79, 88, **89**

III./Gren.Rgt. 440; 33, 35, 62, **71**

4th Battalion The Royal East Kent Regiment (the Buffs) 12, 16, 18, 24, 58, 63, 66, 67, 71, 77, 85, 87

11th Battalion The Parachute Regiment (11 PARA) 17

15./4. Rgt. 'Brandenburg' 43, **43**, 62

22. Infanteriedivision 9

37th Fighter Squadron (USAAF) **36–38** (38), 40, **42**

Aegean Sea 4–5, 7, 13, **23**

air raids 25–26, **55**

air supply drops 72

aircraft 15–16, 17, 18, 24, 25, 26, 35

  Bristol Beaufighter **26**, 29, 40, 49, 89

  Junkers 52; **1**, 16, 43, 59, 62

  Junkers Ju 87 (Stuka) **16**, **35**, **36–38** (38), 40, 74, 75

  Junkers Ju 88; **16**

  Lockheed P-38 Lightning **36–38** (38), 40, 41, **42**

Alinda Cemetery **94**

ammunition dump/logistics camp (Caserna Germè-Esculapio) 32, **33**, 34, **34**

anti-tank guns **15**

Appetici (Mt) 56, 57–58, 60, 62, 63, 64, 66, 71, 77

Aschoff, Hauptmann Philipp 11, **11**, 20, 29

Barrington, Major Ben 57–58, 60

Brandenburg *Fallschirmjäger* 15, 32, 43, **43**, 62

Bristol Beaufighter **26**, 29, 40, 49, 89

British forces 16–18

  commanders 11–12, 21

  numbers of personnel 17–18

  Order of Battle 19

British Intelligence 50

Brittorous, Major-General F. G. R. 'Ben' 11, 43, 48, 91

BYMS 72 (British Yard Minesweeper) 50, **52–54** (54), 55

Campioni, Ammiraglio Inigo 12, 91

*Carlisle*, HMS 38, 40, 41, **41**

chronology of events 8

Churchill, Winston 4, 7, 50

*Citta di Savona* 32

Clark, Lieutenant Clifford **17**, 87

Clidi (Mt) 56, **57**, 58–59, 63, 66–67, 92

commanders 9–12

  quality of officers 21

communications 49, 57, 63, 71, 74, 75, 80, 81, 84, 87, 88

Credential Force 38

Crete 6, 7, 13, 91

decorations 89

Division Brandenburg 13–14, **14**, 15

Dodecanese 4, 5, 6–7, 13, 22, **23**, 91–92

Dörr, Hauptmann Helmut 10, 11, 35, 72, **85**

Egerton, Lieutenant-Colonel S. A. F. S. 64, 85, 90

Enigma 50

escapees from Kos and Leros 90

*Fallschirmjäger* 14, 15, **15**, 32, 33, 35, 43, **43**, 57, 58–59, **59**, 60, 62, 66, **66**, 80, 81

Fiebig, General der Flieger Martin 11, 90

French, Lieutenant-Colonel Maurice **12**, **17**, 24, 60, 64, 66

German forces 13–16

  commanders 9–11, 21

  *Kampfgruppen* (battle groups) 9–11

  numbers of personnel 14, 15

  Order of Battle 19

glide bomb (Henschel Hs 293) 50, **52–54** (54)

graves and memorials **78**, **94**

Greece 5–6, 7

Greek Sacred Squadron (GSS) 17, 58

gun batteries **13**

Hall, Major-General H. R. 12, 48

Hamester, Major Bernhard 11

*Hedgehog* 42, **46**

Hitler, Adolf 7

Iggulden, Lieutenant-Colonel Douglas 63, 66, 84, 87, 90

Italian forces 12, 13, 18–19, 24, 29, 33, 35, 43, 57, 60, 91

Italy

  Armistice 4, **4**, 7, 13

  and Dodecanese 5

  entry to World War II 5

Johnson, Lieutenant E. B. W. (Ted) 57–58, 62, **68–70** (70), 76, 79, 84–85, **91**

Junkers 52; **1**, 16, 43, 59, 62

Junkers Ju 87 (Stuka) **16**, **35**, **36–38** (38), 40, 74, 75

Junkers Ju 88; **16**

Kalpaks 17

Kampfgruppe Aschoff 15, 60

Kampfgruppe Dörr 15, 56, 57

Kampfgruppe Kuhlmann 14, 20, 32

Kampfgruppe Kühne 15, 57, 58–59

Kampfgruppe Müller 71–72

Kampfgruppe Schädlich 15, 56

Kampfgruppe von Saldern 10, 13, 15, 20, 28, 56, 59, 66
*Kampfgruppen* (battle groups) 9–11
Keller, Walter **80**
Kirby, Lieutenant-Colonel Robert 28, 29, 32, 34, 35, 90
Klein, Leutnant 67
Kos 13, 91, 92
  Allied landing **5**, 6
  British defensive plans and preparations 24, 26
  final actions on 40
  see also Operation *Eisbär*
Kriegsmarine 9, 14, 15, 21, 22, 25, 39–40, 41–42, 55, 57, **88**
Kuhlmann, Hauptmann Armin 10, **10**, 11, 32, 35
Kuhlmey, Oberst Kurt **11**
Kühne, Hauptmann Martin 10, 11, **67**
*Küstenjäger* 10, **10**, **14**, 15, 32, 56, 57, 62, 91

landing craft 14, 15, **15**, 21, 22, 28, **33**, 41–42, 48, 56–57, 62, 78–79
Lange, Vizeadmiral Werner **11**, 90
Leggio, Colonello Felice 12, 35, 91
Leros 13, 91, 92
  air raids 25–26
  British defensive plans and preparations 24, 25–26
  change of command at 48–49
  see also Operation *Taifun*
Leros town and castle **49**
Leverette, Major Bill 38, 40, **42**
Levitha 42–48, **44–45**
Lockheed P-38 Lightning 36–38 (38), 40, 41, **42**
Long Range Desert Group (LRDG) 12, 17, **22**, 24, 40, 42, 43, **44–45**, 46–48, **47**, **50**, 56, **56**, 58, 59, 63, 66, 79, 89, 91
Luftwaffe 15–16, **16**, 25, 26, 35, **35**, 40, 43, 49, 58–59, 72, 85–86
see also aircraft

machine guns **17**
Malta 6, 16
maps **21**
  Dodecanese **23**
  Operation *Eisbär* **27**, **30–31**
  Operation *Taifun* **51**, **61**, **65**, **73**, **82–83**

Marinefährprahm (F-lighter) **29**, 39
Mascherpa, Contrammiraglio Luigi **12**, 91
Meraviglia (Mt) 24, 48, 64, 66, 71, 72, 74–75, **76**, **78**, 79, 80, 81, **82–83**, 84, 86–87, 88, 92
Monska, Piepl **80**
Müller, Generalleutnant Friedrich-Wilhelm 9, **9**, **12**, 20, 22, 32, 57, **74**, 81, 88–89, 90
museums **92**

natural resources 7
North Africa 6

Olivey, Captain John R. 46–47, 48, 56
*Olympos* 39, 43
Operation *Eisbär* 28–35, 39
  maps **27**, **30–31**
  plans 20
Operation *Taifun* 50
  12 November 1943; 50, **51**, 55–60
  13 November 1943; 60–64, **61**
  14 November 1943; 64–72, **65**, **68–70** (70)
  15 November 1943; 72–79, **73**
  16 November 1943; 79–89, **82–83**
  maps **51**, **61**, **65**, **73**, **82–83**
  plans 20–22
Order of Battle **19**
ordnance **92**

Phipps, Lieutenant Alan **78**
plans
  British 22, 24
  German 20–22
prisoners of war 7, 39, **39**, 42, 43, **46**, 47, **47**, 48, 56, 66, 67, 79, **85**, **86**, 89, **91**
propaganda photograph **63**

Rachi (Mt) 59, 60, 62, 63, 64, 66, 67, **68–70** (70), 71, 72, 74–77, 79, 84, 85, 87
Ramseyer, Lieutenant-Commander Frank 6, 55, 89
Ransley, Lieutenant Eric J. 58
Read, Major M. R. 75, 76
Rhodes 5, 7, 13, 22, 91
Rickcord, Captain M. B. 80, 84

Ritchie, Lieutenant-Colonel C. W. M. 79, 81, 84, 86
Royal Air Force 6, 17, 18, 24, 25, **26**, 29, 35, 49, 89
Royal Air Force Regiment 17–18
Royal Artillery 17, 18, 56
Royal Navy 6, 18, **18**, 25–26, 38, 39–40, 41, 50, 55–56, 60, 72, 77, 78, 88

Saldern, Major Sylvester von **9**, 10, 71, 80
Schädlich, Leutnant Hans 10, 11, **14**
Schnellboote (E-Boat) **88**
Schrägle, Oberstabsarzt Martin **14**
sea, war at
  4–11 October 1943; 38, 3 9–40, 41
  12–21 October 1943; 41–42
  22–31 October 1943; 48
  1–11 November 1943; 49–50
Sicily 7
Smith, Bill **56**
smokescreens **28**
South African Air Force 25, 26
Special Boat Squadron (SBS) **5**, 6, 12, 17, 24, 40, 58, 59, 63, 79, 89
Sturmdivision Rhodos **4**, 7, 13
Sutherland, Lieutenant Jack 46, 47, 48

Tarleton, Lieutenant-Colonel B. D. 74, 75, 76, 77, 79–81, 84, 86–87, 90
'the Anchor' (Leros) 62, 64, 79–81, 84, 85, 87
Tilney, Brigadier R. A. G. 'Dolly' 12, **12**, 24, 48–49, 60, 64, 67, 72, 74, **74**, 75, 79, 80, 81, 84, 86–88, 91
Turkey 5, 7

*UJ 2111*; 39
*Ultra* 50
United States 7
United States Army Air Force, 37th Fighter Squadron 36–38 (38), 40, **42**

Vaux, Major Hugh M. 28, 32, 35
Voigts, Leutnant **14**

Wandrey, Oberleutnant Max 88, **89**